Divine Mushrooms & Fungi

John W. Allen

Ronin Publishing, INC
Berkeley, California

Eye of the Elephant

A newly developed strain of *Psilocybe cubensis* became known as the "Elephant Dung" strain." John W. Allen had collected several specimens of *Psilocybe cubensis* from elephant dung ball heaps at a Na Muang dung-dump site on Koh Samui Island in the Gulf of Thailand. What was interesting in this grow was the appearance of a group of fresh overnight specimens of *Psilocybe cubensis* that appeared on the 3rd flush of this grow.

For some reason, many cultivators when learning of the 'Elephant Dung' strain of *Psilocybe cubensis*; automatically believed that the species was cultivated indoors in elephant dung. Not so. Growing methods used to cultivate this strain began with PDA agar. After several attempts to fruit this strain in a petri dish, we obtained a rather healthy 3 inch pinner in the agar and then that pinner in the mycelial plate of agar was inoculated by transfer into a plastic bag of pre-sterilized rye berry seeds needed to produce the spawn to grow the strain.

Behold the power of the 'Eye of the Elephant' Dung Strain.

Within 12-days, the mycelium used to produce the spawn had completely colonized the rye berry seeds and was then inoculated into a mycobag of pasteurized rice-paddie straw with pre-sterilized hand-squeezed cow manure compost. Thus a strain was created indoors in a lab.

Divine Mushrooms & Fungi

John W. Allen

Divine Mushrooms & Fungi

Copyright 2014 by John W. Allen
ISBN: 978-1-57951-186-9

Published by
RONIN Publishing, Inc.
P.O. Box 3436
Oakland, Ca 94609

NOTICE TO READER:

This Guide is published under the First Amendment of the Constitution. It not a substitute for professional training and experience. NEVER CONSUME ANY WILD MUSHROOM UNLESS ITS IDENTITY HAS BEEN CONFIRMED BY A SKILLED MYCOLOGIST. The Author and the Publisher of this Guide STRONGLY advise against anyone consuming wild mushrooms and take no responsibility for persons who recklessly do so. ALWAYS GET EXPERT ADVISE from a trained mycologist ON ALL WILD MUSHROOMS *BEFORE* CONSUMING THEM.

Printed in the USA.
Distributed to the trade by Publishers Group West.
www.roninpub.com

Acknowledgements

Thank you to Gastón Guzmán and Alan Rockefeller for taxonomic data for species in the book, and thanks to those who gave supportive comments, expecially Luca Pasquali. Furthermore the author and publisher wish to acknowledge the assistance of Rujiporn Prateepasen at Scientific Technical Research Equipment Center in Chulalongkorn University for her technical assistance in specimen preparation for electron microscope analysis by Prakitsin Sihanonth and the author of this book, along with the staff, students and teachers of Department of Microbiology at Chulalongkorn University in Bangkok. And to Dr. Gastón Guzmán of the Instituto de Ecology, Xalapa, Veracruz, Mexico and noted Bay Area mycologist, Alan Rockefeller for their taxonomic data concerning *Psilocybe caerulescens, Psilocybe weilii, Psilocybe galindoi, Psilocybe tampanensis* and *Psilocybe mexicana.*

The author and publisher thank the following 'shroom voyagers for the use of their unbelievable high quality photographs used in this book: Eric Cifani for his painting of *Xochipilli*: the 'Prince of Flowers.' And for the following whose photos also grace these pages: Caleb Brown, Massive Particles, Professor Smokeface, Jochen Gartz, Prakitsin Sihanonth, Angry Shroom, GGreatOne234, Trappy76, Alan Rockefeller, Steven Peele, Tjakko Stijve, MGW, Oliver of Samui Beach Resort, Grant Trowbridge, Ron Pastorino, Joshua Hutchins, Jason Granquist, Linda Deer, Richard Kneal, Michael Engström, Wipaporn of Koh Samui, Mark Herke, Cyan Shaman, Hans Grootewall. All other photos and art are by John W. Allen.

Ronin extends *a special thanks* to Luca Pasquali and Luca Isabella for catching and correcting spelling of Latin nominclature, which is greatly appreciated.

Dedication

To my colleagues who believed in my research:

Dr, Tjakko Stijve of Nestles, Vevey, Suisse; Dr. Luca Pasquali in Italy, Dr. Gastón Guzmán of the Instituto de Ecologia, Xalapa, Veracruz, Mexico; Dr. Prakitsin Sihanonth of Chulalongkorn University, Bangkok, Thailand; and Dr. Mark D. Merlin of the University of Hawaii at Manoa, Oahu.

Praise for John W. Allen

My good friend, John W. Allen, has monitored and studied entheogenic mushrooms for nearly half of his life. On December 7th of 2012, a new unidentified cold-weather species that stained blue and belonged to the genus *Psilocybe*, was officially named *Psilocybe allenii* Borovička, Rockefeller and P. G. Werner; thus recognizing John's contributions to the field of ethnomycology and then received the taxonomical immortality he deserves within the "Kingdom of the Magic Fungi."

Divine Mushrooms and Fungi summarizes well, with new up-to-date information, how to identify psilocybian fungi, as well as how to dry and preserve them for future studies. Filled with anecdotes, personal vignettes, and bioassays of three species, let John W. Allen become your personal guide; let him share with you his knowledge and how he came to learn all that he could about these mushrooms.

Divine Mushrooms and Fungi is not only lavishly illustrated with more than 200 full color photographs of mushrooms from North America (Canada, the United States, Hawaii); and Mexico, but also features some erotic graphic mushroom art in the book in collaboration between John W. Allen—the author—John's photographs, and the addition of acrylics or airbrush adds to the quality Adisron Junlawanno of Ban Chewang, Koh Samui, Thailand art.

John provides simple safe instructions on how to macroscopically distinguish a deadly poisonous species from that of an active psilocybian species of mushroom. If you truly wish to learn about the magic of these mushrooms. This book, *Divine Mushrooms and Fungi* features more than 200 colored photographs and art by John W. Allen, his friends and his colleagues, presents just a touch—and well beautiful photographs the work—of a whole lifetime.

—Luca Pasquali, Ph.D.
Italia

Table of Contents

Eric Cifani painting of Xochipilli—The Prince of Flowers

Part 1

The 'Shroom Hunter

ONE

Seeking the Magic of the Mushroom

Shroomers often ask me to share my patches of magic. They wonder how I find the special mushrooms, saying they have been searching for years and have not been able to identify them. I tell them to get on a bus, ride it for half an hour, get off and walk their butts off. Sooner or later they will find a lawn or a mulched garden bed with some mushrooms.

I emphasize the need to have a professional verify their finds before putting them into their mouths–like many do. Many people who want to experience the magic and mysticism of these sacred treasures only want to know where they can find them and are unwilling to do a walk-about to find their own private mushroom patches. Mushrooms grow in different habitats. Not all regions have urban 'shrooms, so one must trespass into pasture lands in search of certain species. Then in other regions they grow quite abundantly in man-made environments in public places along both coastal regions of the Americas.

This tale is how I came to Maui, and with no knowledge of *Copelandia* species. I learned about them from strangers I met on the beach and they shared with me some locations on Maui where I might find some. Nothing specific but a single clue to an area where I was told I might find some mushrooms. After that good news from friendly local haoles, I knew it was up to me to find the magic that Maui was known to have.

I began my journey in 1986. Every other day I would hitch a ride up and down Haleakala volcano to Pukalani up into the volcanic-sloped region; that includes the nearby Makawao Rodeo grounds and Kula highway, with pasture lands on both sides of the roadways. That region is referred to as upcountry by locals who, when it gets too hot in Kihei, go up-country to cool off. I made weekly trips to Hana but no ‘shrooms were to be found. Over a three month period I had walked through dozens of fields and found nothing because it was not the right time of the year for where I was looking.

However, ‘shrooms were on other Islands in different locations at different times of the year. It took me nearly three months on Maui to learn their seasons and habitat. To begin with, I first learned that not every field I entered had magic ‘shrooms in the manure of cattle and then after I learned from some friendly people where they suggested I looked, well then “poof”, after three months, there they were. I had finally found my first field of *Copelandia cyanescens* and learned about the magic of the mushrooms in the Hawaiian Islands.

The Thrill of the Hunt

It was just another hot, sunny summer day. I was taking it easy basking in the heat of the scorching noon day sun, while beads of sweat streaked across my brow. Exotic palm trees swayed gently in the breeze. I looked forward to the white foamy surf as it washed ashore upon my bare feet. I was glad I had moved to paradise.

When I arrived on Maui in the summer of 1986, I began a long journey into the world of magic mushrooms and their occurrence in the Hawaiian Islands. To really learn how to find and identify various species of magic mushrooms in Hawaii one needs to try to learn everything about them.

There are at least six active species of psilocybian fungi in Hawaii that grow in the decomposed manure of domesticated four-legged ruminants, like cows, buffaloes, horses, sheep, elephants, and deer. They produce jet black spore deposits and when the stems become damaged from either human handling or from natural elements, then the mushrooms can be easily identified because they stain extremely blue under such conditions.

Copelandia cyanescens from Maui with bluing.

The problem in picking magic mushrooms is the oxidation of psilocine when the flesh of the mushroom is damaged, either from human handling when harvesting specimens from the earth, top-soil, grassy areas in lawns and parks, or in wood chips in mulched garden beds, and in the manure of most four-legged ruminants.

Bluing is the result of improper harvesting of the fungi when lifting them from out of the manure heap.

The best method for picking these manured mushrooms is to use your thumb and forefinger by positioning then at the very base of the mushroom you want to harvest. Never apply pressure directly to the stem of the mushroom and never squeeze the mushroom when lifting it from out of the manure.

If a *Copelandia* species or even an active dung-inhabiting species of *Panaeolus* is damaged, they too will experience the oxidation of psilocine and when that occurs, it causes the mushroom to lose their potency and also possibly infect the clean specimens you have already gathered and placed into your collection container.

When one places such a damaged specimen into a bag of *Copelandia* specimens, or a plastic container, a damaged bluing specimen that lays upon other healthy mushrooms will then infect the other mushrooms in the bag, causing them to also

One dose of freshly harvested *Copelandia cyanescens* with no bluing.

oxidize. I bring this up because over the years I have heard tales from dozens of collectors of these mushrooms about how black and yucky their mushrooms because once they carried them home and tried to dried them. Never put 'shrooms into closed containers or plastic baggie.

Here are two images of how *Copelandia* species should look if properly picked. It took me a few years to learn how to lift them from out of the ground without damaging them and how to clean the manure from the base of the stem.

After the mushroom is lifted from the manure—while still holding it in between your thumb and forefinger—take your bottom two fingers and lightly wrap them around the base of the stem once you lifted it from the manure. Using your pinky and other finger, you can softly and carefully flick off the remaining manure from the base and then lay the mushrooms you have picked all in the same direction in your collection container.

All healthy specimens of *Copelandia cyanescens*, except two bluing mushrooms that had to be tossed.

Anyone interested in these mushrooms should absorb all the knowledge and learn

Observe the cracked, parched and pitted cap of *Copelandia cyanescens*, a common characteristic in *Copelandia* and *Panaeolus* species.

about the environments of the mushroom they are seeking and the flora and fauna of those habitats and the symbiosis of the four-legged ruminants whose dung is responsible for the propagation of the species they are seeking.

While traveling from the airport in Kahului, I observed several street vendors along the highway offering their wares to the traveling tourist. Roadside stands were adorned with such items as Hawaiian T-shirts, sea shells—conch, macramé planters made from seashells and handcrafted bowls and hats made from the fronds and leaves of exotic palms. Flower peddlers also offered fragrant lei's made from Plumeria, Ginger, or Gardenia.

The ride from the airport to Kihei was enjoyable. I rode passed my first sugar cane field and realized that this was the first real sugar cane field I had ever seen except for the ones in the film "Diamond Head" starling Charlton Heston. The stalks of the sugar cane were over 12 feet tall and blowing in the wind, all in unison. I noticed various roadside stalls offering local fruits intended for tourist consumption. On Maui, many roads once offered the weary visiting traveler as well as local inhabitants, a chance to stop and purchase fresh fruit right from the fields where they grew.

Such roadside fruit stands offer fresh pineapples, coconuts, coconut milk, mangoes, papayas, bananas, star fruit, passion fruit, guava, and punene—pear—cactus. If you're thirsty, fruit juice smoothies and shave ice are refreshing and quite popular, but if you want a real treat, Hawaii's famous Macadamia nuts are always available. After a few years on Maui, ordinances were passed, as they were on Oahu that prohibited many local Hawaiians from vending merchandise and fresh fruit to the tourists who visit the Islands.

I finally arrived in Kihei and made temporary living arrangements, then went down to the beach by the Royal Mauiian Apartment complex to relax while lying in the hot sand at Kamaouli I Beach. After several months at that beach, I made a few friends. It was at this very beach that I learned that the magical island of Maui, the land of Hounoli, was definitely much more than just the land of rainbows, friendly natives, fragrant flowers and the hula.

On this first day of taking in the sun while at the beach, I immensely enjoyed the luxury of watching the many beautiful women who graced the beach in their scantily clad island styled G-stringed bikinis. Out in the water I watched an array of about ten or more small boats comprising a fleet of moored trimarans—large catamarans—and various one and two-masted sailboats and a single Catalina gently swaying to and from in the warm water.

The moored vessels were awaiting the daily arrival of tourists who would venture forth on a voyage to the volcanic cap of Molikini, an extinct volcano near west Kihei, or Olowalu—two great snorkeling locations where exotic fish and coral can be viewed au natural. Besides snorkeling, other popular water sports for Hawaii's many visitors include: swimming, water skiing, jet skiing, wind surfing and surfing. Local surfers and surfers from Europe and Australia loved to pick and eat magic mushrooms prior to surfing. Surfing on 'shrooms in Hawaii was reported in 1974 by Dr. Steven H. Pollock.

When one has nothing to do except lounge around on a beach all day, basking in the heat of the hot blazing sun, maybe enjoying a shave ice or ice tea or even a fruit juice smoothie is surely recommended. Or maybe a plain glass of iced lemonade will cool one off. I bought a snow cone of shave ice and then took a brief cooling off in the salty water for about 20 minutes or so, then returned to my blanket to dry myself off after hosing down in the public shower and sat down, staring back towards the ocean while viewing the boats in front of me from the beach.

I proceeded to turn away from gazing at the boats in the water and looked upwards towards the west slopes of Haleakala—House of the Sun. Haleakala is a dormant volcano that dominates at least one half of the island and offers to tourists one of the most spectacular views found on Maui; a crater that offers the most beautiful sunrises and sunsets views in the entire world; and at 10,000 feet you can almost see forever.

As the sun continued to soak me in, I couldn't help but overhear a conversation that was taking place not more than five feet from where I lay. Looking over to my right, I noticed a small group of locals who were downing their beers and passing pakalolo—marijuana—amongst themselves. I picked up little bits and pieces of their conversation from a local haole who was discussing a possible trip to Hana for the purpose of obtaining some Hawaiian Magic Mushrooms.

The locals had referred to the mushrooms as both "cone heads" and "gold caps", both local epithets given to Hawaiian mushrooms by 'shroom lovers who lived in the islands. Folk names are common among amateur mycophiles on the mainland that live in the Pacific Northwest and the Gulf Coast regions of the United States and from the conversation I was now eavesdropping on, I guessed that this was also true for Maui.

Yum! That got me to thinking about how I would go about finding magic mushrooms on Maui. I wondered if it was safe to wander around on private properties.

Stimulated and excited beyond my wildest imagination over the topic of their discussion, I decided to introduce myself to this small group of locals as an amateur expert in the field identification of entheogenic mushrooms. During the next few hours, I learned from these strangers that Maui's "magic mushrooms" were very common after heavy rainfalls and most definitely constituted a part of the drug subculture that existed here in Hawaii.

After a while, I asked my new found friends where I might be able to obtain some of these interesting "gold capped" mushrooms. I asked if anyone would be interested in taking me on a field trip to search for them. I explained that I would be more than willing to pay expenses such as gas and lunch if someone would be willing to show me where they grew and what they looked like. Unfortunately no one was interested in leaving the warmth and peacefulness of the hot sunny beach for the wet swampy pasture lands I so graciously sought.

One of the locals named Marc was a cook at the Island Fish House. He told me that I should go up Haleakala along the Kula highway until I came upon the Ching store. Just beyond the store I would find several open fields where cows grazed on each side of the highway. Marc said that all I would have to do is search for a cow pie and I would find more mushrooms than I could ever imagine. He said that if I were to continue along Kula road past the 'Ching' store, I would eventually come across Ulupalakua ranch, an area covering some 30,000 acres, which play host to thousands of scattered dung-heaps, many of which were undoubtedly home to the "magic mushrooms" I was so interested in obtaining.

A local biker named Chet joined our small group and he suggested that I should travel to "Heavenly Hana" located on the other side of the island. Hana is one of the rainy areas on Maui

Massless Particles

Lyons Hill fungi habitat in Hana extends for miles into the interior.

Fresh sub-bleached caps of *Psilocybe cubensis* across the grass.

and is well known amongst both locals and tourists from Australia as an ideal location for picking "magic mushrooms." Chet confided to me that there were numerous pastures and paddocks between Hana and the seven "sacred" pools. Chet said he had picked there before and on one occasion had collected over eight pounds of mushrooms in a single day. He said that "magic mushrooms" could be picked all year long when the weather conditions were right.

Chet said his favorite picking area was in a spot off of the Hana Highway at the top of "Lyons Hill." Marc agreed with Chet and said that I would have no trouble in locating this hill because the top of it was graced with a giant stone cross. Access to "Lyons Hill" is public and both sides of the short winding road leading up to the top are excellent fields for picking "magic mushrooms."

After a little while, another doobie was rolled and passed around and I joined in. I thanked Marc and Chet and the rest of my new found friends for making my day, and I decided I was definitely going to travel to Hana in the morning and see if I could find these elusive basidiomes which had captivated my reason for wanting to stay in Maui.

The following day, I awoke to the sound of roosters crowing and the sweet fragrance of Plumeria drifting through the air. With much enthusiasm I proceeded to ready myself for my pilgrimage to Hana by packing my back pack with the necessary equipment needed for gathering magic mushrooms; a pair of scissors, paper bags, my camera with some extra rolls of film, and my sleeping bag, since I thought I might camp out in Hana for the night. I then set on down the road towards my destination, making one stop at the Paradise Fruit Stand in Kihei for a 'mango smoothie,' 2 fresh ripe mangoes, 4 bottles of water, and a papaya for the road.

John with tray of 'shrooms

TWO

On the Road Again

Hitchhiking in Maui is illegal. So I should not have been surprised that as soon as I put my thumb out for a ride, an officer of the law appeared out of nowhere to inform me that it was illegal to hitchhike. He warned me that if he caught me with my thumb out again I could be fined $400 for hitchhiking. The officer was friendly, smiling all the time as he talked to me. He told me if I were to just stand along the road with my arms crossed someone would likely come along and offer me a ride. As the officer left, I cussed under my breath, "Shit! Yeah! I'm sure! I could be here all fuckin' day long 'fore I get a ride," however, within five minutes after the officer had driven away, a car pull over and offered me a ride.

Amazed, I immediately hopped in and an elderly Hawaiian fisherman told me he would drop me off on the other side of Puunene, near the Hana highway. Twenty minutes later, I was dropped off next to a sugar cane field along the Hana highway. I could hear the sound of the wind as it whistled through the sugar cane, which was flowing quite freely through the wind. The cane appeared to be 10 to 12 feet tall, since I couldn't see the top of Haleakala because the sugar cane interfered with the view.

I stood along the highway, folded my arms, and awaited another ride. Before too long, a car pulled over and a real cute girl leaned out of the window; ask me where I was going and told me to hop in. This time my hosts were a young married couple named Jay and Lori who explained they were only going about four miles down the road to a club called Charlie's Tavern in Paia. I would have no trouble hitching a ride from there to Hana, they said.

Professor Smokeface.

Maui Wowie from Paia, Maui.

I was in the car for about half a minute when Lori turned to me and asked me if I would like to smoke some "Maui Wowie." Lori said that some of their friends had grown the herb in Huelo, down by the sea. Before I could answer, she handed me a lit pipe that she apparently had been cuffing in her hands while checking me out. I took the pipe and then proceeded to smoke.

As I passed the pipe back to Lori in the front seat, I gasped and choked from the big pig toke that I had taken. Both Jay and Lori burst out laughing at me for being a pig. Jay glanced at me through his rear view mirror and I could see him laughing. "Some potent shit, huh!" he exclaimed and I nodded my head in agreement while I choked and gagged from the smoke.

Since I realized my ride was cool, I decided to tell Jay and Lori of my pilgrimage to Hana and asked them if they knew of any spots where I might find some magic mushrooms. Jay and Lori both reassured me that my friends in Kihei had not steered me wrong and that Hana was definitely the place to go if I wanted to find some magic mushrooms.

As Lori drew a map of the Hana area, Jay explained what lay ahead for me as I traveled down the Hana highway. Jay said that after Paia, the road to Hana—the "Heavenly Highway"—would be straight until I reached the twenty-mile marker. There, at Twin Falls, the road twists and bends crazily along the cliffs. Lori added that from Huelo going eastward toward Hana, I would soon smell the dense fragrance of flowers and foliage emulating from the lush tropical rain forests along the highway.

Jay said there were many pastures and plenty of green-ferned fertile valleys along the route, with more than fifty one lane bridges that crossed deep ravines and gushing stream beds. The left side of the highway is a drop-away coastline supported by jagged lava-rocks, and very beautiful pounding surf. On my right, I was told, at several of the bridges, I would see cascading waterfalls, and thickets of bamboo, Guava and Rose Apple trees with ripe fruit ready for picking and eating. They said there were Eucalyptus trees and, if I walked along the road, I would probably find some ripe, little red chilies.

Lori said I should check out the Seven "Sacred" Pools of Kipahulu on the other side of Hana. Beautiful waterfalls fill most of them and, although the rocks at the pools are slippery, the chilly pools are ideal for swimming as well as tripping. Lori said this would be a splendid place to spend the day high on mushrooms.

It took us about 10 minutes to reach Paia, and by then I was really buzzed by the four tokes of "Maui Wowie" that my ride had shared with me. As Jay drove into the small seaside community of Paia, I couldn't help but notice the many brightly painted storefront shops that graced the right side of my window view that were very reminiscent of the bright colorful storefront shops of the Haight-Ashbury district in San Francisco.

"Well, this is as far as we go" Jay exclaimed as he pulled into the parking lot of Charlie's Tavern, which featured live music and dancing. It was at that moment that I noticed a ten-foot high fence layered

Massless Particles

A Valley habitat for *Copelandia* species near Hana, Maui.

with beautiful vines of pinkish-violet flowers with palm-sized heart- shaped leaves. They extended the length of the whole parking lot. I asked Lori if she knew what kind of flowers they were.

Baby Hawaiian Woodrose Vines growing in Paia, Maui.

Once again Lori laughed and said, "You're not going to believe this but those are `Baby Hawaiian Woodrose'" (*Argyreia nervosa*). Lori explained that one of the waitresses at Charlie's was cultivating them and exporting them to head shops on the mainland. Jay told me the seeds from these vines were similar in effect to LSD but they were not illegal to possess.

"If someone were to rip off your crop of Woodrose, you could call the police and they would attempt to find out who ripped you off." "Of course" Jay continued, "you can't call the cops if someone were to rip off your field of smoke."

As I got out of the car, I thanked Jay and Lori for the ride, the smoke, and all the information they had impounded into my circuits. As I watched Jay and Lori slowly disappear into Charlie's, I walked over and took some photographs of the vines, their flowers and some seeds. I knew I would return and pick a few.

So happy was I that I danced over to the highway singing "Lodi". Again I stood at the road, crossed my arms, wondering what new and exciting adventures laid before me. I had a dream that I would one day find my own Woodrose patch as this plant was introduced into the Hawaiian Islands from India to be used as decorative floral arrangements. I even envision myself kneeling down looking over my very own first big score of Baby Hawaiian Woodrose Seeds.

I guess it must have been at least fifteen minutes before I got tired of standing in the hot sun, so I started to hike down the road, turning around every now and then, watching as a long steady flow of cars kept passing me. I wondered why I was having such a hard time getting a ride, but it didn't bother me. I just kept walking. After about ten minutes, I noticed an unusual graveyard on the left side of the road. Each tombstone was adorned with colorful flowers and Japanese lanterns. The first tombstone I saw was rather large, with the name "Toyota" chiseled into it. I laughed to myself and wondered if an automobile were buried there.

Continuing down the road past the graveyard; I could barely make out a figure ahead of me, which appeared to be another hitchhiker carrying what looked like a surfboard on his shoulder. I caught up with the surfer, a young local Hawaiian boy named Kimo. He was friendly and asked my name and where I was from. I told him that I had just moved to Maui from Oregon, and I was now living in Kihei. I said I was on my way to Hana to pick some of Maui's world famous Hawaiian magic mushrooms.

So it was no surprise when Kimo informed me that I did not have to go all the way to Hana in order to find some magic mushrooms. He described an open field that stretched for about two miles along the left side of the Hana Highway, a location where Kimo and his friends had just harvested magic mushrooms from a few days earlier.

Baby Hawaiian Woodrose flower in Paia, Maui.

Seeds of Baby Hawaiian Woodrose from Paia, Maui.

Kimo said I should watch for a leveled area with about 9 cows in the field. On a later visit to the same field I did count the cattle and there were exactly 9 cattle in the field! Kimo said I would know the field by two signs. One that warned there could be kite flyers, casting large giant rectangular box-kites over the cliff along the pasture. Kimo said that the field was located just above Ho'o'kipa State Park, a popular wind surfing area, often frequented by surfers from all over the world. He reaffirmed the knowledge that many surfers from other continents came to Hawaii seeking magic mushrooms and surfing. They claimed the mushrooms enabled the surfers to become one with the waves while under their influence.

Kimo said I would have no trouble in finding the pasture. He described a single wooden shack that stood erect in the middle of the field situated about 100 feet from a cliff overlooking the ocean. He said that from the cliff, I could watch the many multi-colored sails from the windsurfers as their sailboards caught the winds to glide to and fro in the water below.

Mark D. Merlin

The author with a large bag of Baby Hawaiian Woodrose pods and seeds.

As we walked down the highway, I realized that it had been about 40 minutes since Jay and Lori had dropped me off and I still had not gotten a ride. Kimo said not to worry, people were friendly on Maui and I would get a ride sooner or later. He turned into a driveway where he lived. As we parted, I thanked him for turning me on to his mushroom patch and continued on down the road.

After about fifteen minutes, I noticed that the residential area on the left side of the highway was thinning out and to my right; fields of sugar cane continued along the roadway. I came to a turn in the road and as I followed it around the bend, I spied Mama's Fish House where I stopped to fill my canteen with fresh water.

Just past Mama's, the ocean came into view and after walking for about another twenty minutes, I saw the wind surfers' sails out in the ocean. In the distance I could make out the shape of the shack that Kimo had told described. I had finally arrived.

John with Terrance.

THREE

Toads and Magic Fungi

As I crept closer, the shack grew larger. It was not a wooden as Kimo had described it, but was constructed of large concrete blocks. It was about 20 feet by 8 feet with a wooden roof.

I climbed over the gate and wandered towards the shack, as I surveyed the pasture in search of cow pies. Making my way to the front of that stone shack, I found myself facing the ocean directly in front and below me. I thanked the spirits of the four corners for welcoming me into their space.

The first dozen or so dung-heaps I espied were void of mushrooms. I thought the field had been picked out by other 'shroomers. Or perhaps the mushroom season had not yet started. I felt a tinge of disappointment creep over me because I hadn't found any mushrooms.

The grass in the pasture was about eight inches high, which I kicked aside to see what might be hiding in it. I noticed an off-white glint in the grass, so I bent over to move the grass aside to see what it might be. It was the moment I had been waiting for! There in the middle of a cow pie, were two medium-sized small mushrooms protruding up through the

Ho'o'kipa, a shack on Maui as seen from the Hana Highway.

The author standing in front of Ho'o'kipa,

grass. I pulled some of the grass away to get a better look.

The two mushrooms were small with thin stems and a few splotches of blue were scattered across the cap of one. The other smaller capped mushroom had a light azure-blue stain running down the length of its stem. The bluing on these two mushrooms occurred from natural elemental damage such as either wind or cattle kicking them.

My search for the magic mushrooms of Hawaii that I so diligently sought had finally arrived. The mushrooms were directly in front of me as if it had been preordained that I would find them exactly where I had found them there on Maui. Seeing the small blue-staining splotches on the cap and stem of these two mushrooms were fruiting in manure, I realized I had finally found fresh specimens of *Copelandia cyanescens.*

With care, I slowly pulled the 'shrooms out of the cow pie. Kneeling in the grass, I slowly scanned to the left and to the right. My eyes took a while to adjust to the bright gleam of the sun in the grass. On both sides of me, I saw several more cow pies with mushrooms growing in them. Startled by my discovery, I retrieved a plastic container from my back pack and began to pick the mushrooms.

Splotches of bluing from natural elemental damage on cap and stem of *Copelandia cyanescens.*

One cow pie had more than 25 mushrooms growing from out of it with caps ranging in size from a quarter of an inch up to one and a half inches in diameter.

Later collections revealed that a single cow-pie could produce from two to three fresh flushes with as

More than 25 specimens of *Copelandia cyanescens* in a single cow pie.

Later collections revealed that a single cow pie can produce 50 to 200 fresh mushrooms.

Since the mushrooms I had just picked appeared to have been drying in the sun for a half an hour or so, many of their caps were cracked and wrinkled; some displayed bright tinges of azure blue-turquoise deep-sea green splotches running along the edges of the caps towards its center. The stems of the mushrooms were thin, ranging from about 1 to 5 inches in length. In less than five minutes the stems of the mushrooms I had just picked were turning extremely blue, verifying their psychoactivity.

I slowly stood up. I had picked over 80 mushrooms from just five cow pies. Excited as I was, I thought I should check out the rest of the field to see just how far their growth spread.

At the other end of the field, there was a drop leading into a small valley that extended down to the ocean. Wherever I walked there were multitudes of cow pies, all with mushrooms growing from them.

It was about 10:30 AM and I knew how my day was going to turn out. I would spent the day picking, taking dips in the ocean and relaxing in the sun and the shade. Then I would set up my campsite for the night in the shack and bio-assay my fresh mushrooms. I had a drink of water from my canteen and continued to pick all the mushrooms I could find, spending most of the day on my hands and knees—avoiding the curious cows who wondered what I was doing..

I came upon a magnificent toad standing guard over a lonely bluing specimen of *Copelandia cyanescens*. The presence of bluing in this species is so spectacular that it provides nature with its own natural indication of the presence of psilocine in this species and other members of the genus *Copelandia*.

The genus *Bufo* includes more than two-hundred species and *Bufo marinus*—the 'sugar' cane toad—was introduced to the Hawaiian Islands to reduce sugar cane beetles and insects. Today, cane toads are considered as pests. In the wild, they are opportunistic carnivores that non-selectively consume invertebrates—bugs—but also eats vertebrates—frogs and snakes—and plants; reproducing any time when warm enough; laying thousands of eggs. In Hawaii, dogs and cats have been adversely affected since they have no natural immunity to bufotoxin when a domesticated animal licks a toad out of curiosity.

The epithet "toadstool" was originally used to identify any wild mushrooms considered non-edible, toxic, hallucinogenic, or poisonous, while the epithet "mushroom" is usually associated with fungi considered to be edible and used as a food. In medieval times, toads were associated with European witches who allegedly used their venom in potions and rituals. Another toad, *Bufo alvarius,* known as the "Sonoran" Desert Toad or "Colorado River" toad, contains 5-MEO-DMT. It is a potent hallucinogen known in the Amazon as both Yopo snuff and as Cohba snuff in the West Indies.

Over 200 specimens were harvested from this manured area around a palm tree.

I stood amazed as I wandered in the land of fairies, toads and magic fungi, knowing that great expectations were happening in this magical garden of joy.

As the day wore on, the heat become increasingly unbearable. The sun was hot and I was showing signs of sunburn on my arms and face. When I decided to call it quits at about 5:00 PM I had filled 6 medium-sized plastic containers with the mushrooms.

Slowly making my way back towards the shack standing by the edge of the cliff, I could see numerous colonies of the mushrooms in the ground looking up at me as I walked. I was sore from bending over and kneeling all day. I wanted to relax. I hoped the shack would be a comfortable place to bed down for the night.

The view from in front of the shack was spectacular. Wind surfers zipped back and forth. The coast line on both sides of me was really fantastic. I walked down the side of the cliff and sat upon the slated lava-rock bed by the ocean's edge, watching the crabs scurry in and out of the crevices and nooks in the rock. The high tide waves cascaded up onto the side of the cliff, splashing and spraying humongous mists of water towards me, splashing upwards over 40 feet high—a natural blow hole.

I walked back up to the shack and looked inside, hoping it was livable. There was a 2 x 4 across the front of where the door had once hung. It was probably placed there to keep the cattle out. Inside it smelled musty. I took incense sticks out of my back pack, lit and placed them in a crevice in the concrete block wall.. I moved aside some big blocks in the center of the floor. "Oh!" Something behind the blocks moved, startling me. I jumped backwards about two feet, falling to the stone floor.

Two large toads like the one I found guarding the bluing *Copelandia* were huddled among the blocks in a darkened corner. I slowly pushed them out of the door with my feet. I did not need uninviting guests during my overnight visit. These toads, which are common in the Islands, are *Bufo*—cane—toads or *Bufo marinus.* They secret a poison from their glands that can be toxic to humans and animals. The warts, glands, and skin of one species, *Bufo alvarius* contains an entheogenic compound; primarily, 5-MEO-DMT.

In Hawaii, the sun usually sets at about 7 PM. At about 6:30 I cleaned several of the fresh mushrooms, intending to eat some that very night. I took out 14 mushrooms from one of the containers. That would be my dose for the evening. I stepped outside to photograph the dosage so I would remember the experience. At the last minute, I added 6 more mushrooms for my voyage.

Copelandia cyanescens and Bufo Toad in Ho'o'kipa, Maui.

After cleaning the manure from 20 mushrooms of various sizes, I laid my sleeping bag out, opened my back pack, set up my radio, along with my canteen, flashlight and a few other items necessary to feel comfortable throughout the evening.

I ate the mushrooms slowly, one at a time until they were all gone. Within 15 minutes I had consumed the last mushroom. It had gotten completely dark inside and outside of the shack. The only light was a misty haze that emanated from the front door of the shack. The door looked directly towards the starry sky and the light from the stars reflected brightly on the ocean below me. The crescent moon was behind the shack, not providing any light. I could even see phosphorus floating on the jammies.

The stars were glistening brightly, appearing very intense and thick in the sky. I felt the crest of ripples beginning to surge within me from the mushrooms. I laid down on my sleeping bag before I took off. The effect of being alone in that room, completely surrounded by darkness, with just my radio and a few *Bufo* toads hopping around somewhere was most exotic.

Even before I had even hit the 20-minute marker leading to the commencement of the mushrooms', I saw light visuals of grid lines approaching me at an alarming speed. Not as fast as the speed of light. I could see colored grids constantly changing as they neared me, went through me, and even passed by me and they still kept coming, pulsating to the beat and rhythm of my heart. Pounding my mind with each throb of their texture, I saw the light disappearing completely in pure darkness as they had begun their attack on my conscious soul.

I leaned over lightly to tuned my radio to KAOI FM, which is owned by Don Henley, formerly of the Eagles. I was beginning to enjoy the oncoming euphoria that was coming on in waves. The music was just what I needed. In Hawaii, KAOI FM Radio is referred to locally as "No KAOI"—Number one— the best FM Rock Station in Hawaii.

I was in total darkness. I could see into my mind; I could see myself inside my brain. The grids of color were slowly becoming mandalas, echoes of my memories. I saw myriad images of myself reflecting in and out of my vision, pulsating throughout my body. They directed my every thought and the means to process those thoughts.

After what seemed like ten minutes but was more likely a few seconds, I saw myself laying on my sleeping bag in wonderment as multiple layers of myself looked back at me, repeating the imagery over and over and over. I again experienced the power of the mushrooms as the visuals increased in their speed as they approached, faster than I had seen in years.

I heard a sound. Paranoia came out of nowhere as I heard a croaking sound nearby. I wondered if it might be the two toads I had booted out of the shack. Perhaps they could turn me into a prince I mused. That was when I knew this "trip" would be an intense visual and most rewarding experience

The average dosage of *Copelandia cyanescens* with ruler to show size.

I could actually feel my thoughts as living colors. They allowed me to sense that I that I knew where I was at and that where I was at was exactly where I needed to be. I believed the incoming visuals I was experiencing, rapid as they were, had provided me with millions of minuscule particles of living colors, and in each color I could feel their presences inside my soul.. I knew these mushrooms were enabling me to feel every vibrant colored I needed to feel. I felt the colors I saw under the influence of these sacred mushrooms there at Ho'o'kipa, Maui.

Graphic depiction of the author's mind while experiencing the effects of the mushrooms.

I thanked the god's for leading me to this special place, although every now and then I could smell the mildew and mustiness of the stone shack, the odor did not bother me, but it did remind me that I was most fortunate to have a temporary place to grace the night with my presence. For some reason there were two strips of slat-like boards across the center of the door on an angle. I thought that it may have once been used as a shelter for a few cattle that needed to get out of the rain. But then again, I wondered why they were blocking the entrance into the door. I was able to just walk under them by lowering my head.

The pasture along the ocean side was a long strip of land with cliffs that ran along the ocean front for at least a quarter mile down the Hana Highway. There were surfers below and the kite flyers also hopped the fence as I had. The Kite-fliers who were there when I arrived that morning had a second person to hold them down on the ground because the big box kites could blow them out to sea. They were at the south end of the pasture leading back to the Highway.

The effects of the mushrooms in my mind became like Big-Bang-Boom, Big-Badda-Boom. In rapid secession, they hit me in waves. I was finally one with everything in my environment and in my world.

I was moved by the resonating echo of Bing-Bang-Boom repeating that sound over and over and over, like a massive thunderstorm clapping. As I heard the colors and saw the sounds, the massive movements of visuals kept coming at me, directly splattering into my face, endlessly in rapid secession.

The visions spoke to me. I heard the color of the music surrounding and engulfing my very spirit in synchronicity and I heard it shout out my mantra, "God is a plant known as the Earth. I had not been to this dimensional level of consciousness since my first mushroom experience ten years earlier. I was proud that

My voyage on the 'shrooms presented visuals displaying never ending grids of colors.

Mushroom Visuals.

Imagine the images undulating towards you.

the *Copelandia* species had steered me in the right direction. This journey made this voyage at Ho'o'kipa one that I would not soon forget.

I was still seeing multiple layers of myself reverberating to and fro, and it was then that I knew that I was on my way to "Lala land" and this indeed was about to become a very intense voyage into my subconscious soul and mind.

FOUR

Psychedelic Visions

Within 20 minutes my visuals had become so intense that I closed my eyes hoping to make the rapid succession of the visuals slow down, but there they were, inside of me as well as outside of me. My eye lids felt as if they were being sprayed by a fine mist, a mist of intricate dotted minute particles of soft colors, colors that were geodesic patterns enveloping my whole vision.

The colors exploded endlessly. They were so explicit and clear, yet sharp and piercing, that I had to open my eyes within a few seconds after each moment from the time I closed them. The colors were like lasers dancing to the rhythm of the music which was emanating from my radio. They contracted and expanded with each breath I took. Then each molecule of sound that I experienced continued to explode in front of me into millions of contracting particles of vivid colors. The lines of color that I experienced were definitely grid-like in their structure.

I could envision orgasmic creations of nebulae and star clusters that began formulating in my mind. When I gazed out the door of the shack, I noticed that the water from the ocean's edge had slowly ebbed itself towards the bottom of my door where I was laying, as if it were going to roll on in and touch the tips of my toes. What was really strange is that I knew that the water outside my door was about a hundred feet outwards in front of me, and 40 feet down below me, yet the effects from being isolated and surrounded by total darkness, caused a deprivation of natural light that added to my hallucinatory visual panorama.

Graphic interpretation of mushroom visuals.

As I came to the realization that the oncoming water couldn't reach or touch me, I slowly attempted to raise my eyes towards the center of the door—it was like a hole in space and I could only see the star filled night. As I did so, I noted the visual effect of total darkness with only a door filled with stars from the sky above me. I knew that if I were to suddenly get up, something which I knew I couldn't do at the time, go to the door and take one step beyond (a pun), I would have forever fallen into the void of heaven. I wondered if I were to come back on another night and didn't eat any mushrooms, if the room and the stars instill in me the same effects I experienced on that night.

For the next 20 minutes or so, or maybe it was 2 hours, I sat and listened to my music and gazed at my friends, the stars. As I looked out my window of heaven, nothing else in life existed in or out of that room, except me, my music, the intense on rush of visuals that kept exploding against my face; and my stars.

I stepped outside to get a breath of fresh air and check on the weather because the Maui clouds were fogging my doorway to the stars. I took a look-see behind the shack, when suddenly to see a crescent moon appeared from nowhere, exploding into hundreds of little sibling crescent moons, all in unison and a domino effect imploded outwards towards me in several different directions at the same time. They were extending downwards from the sky and heading directly towards me and the Earth. Each branch of the moon became a replication of itself like the many dangling hanging branches on a Banyan tree seeking the shelter of the Earth from the oncoming storm.

My visuals were again more pronounce. I thought I was really doing okay until about 10:30 PM when the batteries in my radio expired. I had brought extra batteries with me, so I sat up as the visuals were still coming at me in all directions. They were like echoes bouncing off of me and every time I looked or glanced in another direction, the visuals would change their color, and position their flow in tune to every movement I made as I played tag with it, following their pathway in unison with mine.

Yet, again my time line became distorted so minutes seemed like hours and an hour seemed like a minute. The colors of my visuals changed from a dark blue hue that I saw when I looked up at the moon into a red and blue like checker board that began to melt. My body felt quite rubbery. I melted at different angles within the visuals that were again engulfing my very essence. I knew at that time that when I laid down, the visuals would mellow out and slow to a smooth flow. Now that I stood up, they seemed to know I had arisen and the rushes began all over; and yet I still enjoyed the psilophorian effects that were still very overwhelming.

I sat up and turned my flash light on and dug around in my back pack for the new batteries I had brought. Upon fixing the radio, I turned the flash light off. I looked out the door again to see if the effects were the same as earlier.

Á crescent moon descends and replicates from the sky towards the Earth.

My opened doorway into the

Geodesic visual 'shroom patterns in a continuous flow.

universe had a wonderful surprise for me. There in the window of the door frame stood the big dipper. I laughed quite hysterically at the site of it, for it appeared to be dipping into the ocean. As I gazed upon it I wondered if it was getting a refill, and if tomorrow it would dump it's fill on Lahaina or Hana. I laughed again and again, until I began to hurt from my laughing so much at nothing.

After a little time passed most of my hallucinations slowed down. The stars in the doorway faded as dark clouds invaded their view of the island. I could smell the approaching rain in the sky, and I could hear thunder and see lightning off in the distance. As the lightning grew closer and closer I realized its power and wondered if I were in danger. I thought of Dorothy and Toto being blown away from Kansas and back and wondered if the concrete shack where I was holed up could survive the coming storm.

With the thought of a storm approaching my world, I looked out and there appeared in the sky, some very bright flashes of intense lightning and I said out loud, "I hope it doesn't hit me." Then I thought about what I had said and burst into an uncontrollable surge of laughter at the thought of being stuck by lightening. "Well" I thought, "if it does, I hope I don't feel it." At that thought I went off the deep end into hysterics. I could not believe that I had said that, let alone have thought of something so silly.

At that moment I heard a big thunder clap of sound emanating from the sky over the ocean and I felt that my stone shack suddenly transform into a bamboo shack being flung into the atmosphere like Dorothy being flung into Oz when her farm home was hit by a tornado.

By one o'clock I was ready to go to sleep. I had come to the conclusion that I had a most unique and beautiful experience. I couldn't wait to get back to my home in Kihei and tell my many new found friends of my expedition and voyage on the sacred mushrooms I had found on my own. That was the full Maui experience, an experience that everyone should participate in by coming to Maui for the greatest educational experience of their lives.

That night I had definitely experienced a symbiotic relationship with the mushrooms, the land, and with the spirit of Mother Maui herself. I even heard the ali nui whistling in the wind.. I slept like a prince that night and the following morning when I awoke, I cleaned up my mess and picked up all of my litter, collected my six plastic containers of 'shrooms, and walked out of my magic door across the pasture heading home.

I saw the Big Dipper dip down into the Pacific catching rainbows of colorful hues, splashing them all over.

I slowly made my way to the gate, making a mental note to come back the next day, because I noticed a lot of mushrooms had sprung up during the night from the rain transmitting a message

The shack was a "Doorway to the Stars."

to me saying "don't forget us, come back again when you can."

I remembered that just before I fell asleep I saw particles coming at me that reminded me of snowflakes of many colors. The onslaught of these individual molecular-like geodesic structures were that they were symmetrically perfect in every way, even when I closed my eyes or opened them, these kaleidoscopic visuals bled into my soul. I loved the patterns that I experienced that evening. I created a graphic interpretation of that snowflake image that invaded my time and space. When I say snowflake, it is because each individual image was different as the time it took to come and go through me.

Snowflake reflection fractal graphic designed mushroom visual.

These morsels were harvested in under a half an hour of picking.

I went back the next day and I collected two more containers of some really fresh healthy specimens of *Copelandia cyanescens*. By the time I arrived at the Ho'o'kipa patch, there were about 9 young adults in the field, two flying giant kites with two friends holding the kite flyers to the ground so the persons guiding the kite would not be lifted into the air over the ocean. The other five were bent over picking mushrooms. After a half an hour I left because I did not want to meet anyone that morning. They were friendly, so I talked with them about the mushrooms and their relationship with the mushrooms. The young 'shroomers kids were all right.

John and Andrew Weil.

FIVE

Voyages Beyond Gravity

My first mushroom experience was in the early 1960s in California when I consumed about half a gram of a possible piece of a stem that may or may not have been *Psilocybe cubensis*. At the time, I did not realize that it was not enough of a dose to feel the little known effects I had heard about.

The early trip was followed in 1972 in Chicago when I was given a couple of psilocybine capsules, which I was told I could smoke. Again, nothing happened.

Later my wife and I took a trip in 1974 on hallucinogenic mushrooms claimed to have been smuggled into Oregon from Mexico. They were sealed in a tin can like that of the U.S. Army's K-Ration and C-Ration tins. When I opened the can I found it contained chunks of frozen reddish to a brownish-colored syrupy substance-like liquid mixture.

I had been told to keep the mushrooms in the freezer because if they were left out, the frozen mushrooms and the psilocybine in them would melt and fall into the settling liquid in the bottom of the tin. I was told that eating a spoonful of the syrup from the bottom of the can would get me extremely high.

Analysis of those 'shrooms by Pharm Chem Labs in Palo Alto, California revealed that they were a grocery store species of edible mushrooms that had been laced with LSD and coated with PCP to hide the effects of the acid and had been mixed into the can before it was hermetically sealed. I was told that the mushrooms had been smuggled into America from Mexico.

Psilocybian Consciousness Spreads

In the 1960s college students discovered magic mushrooms thanks to Timothy Leary who first ate mushrooms while on vacation in Cuernavaca, Mexico. Tim brought the knowledge back to Harvard University and soon word of 'shrooms spread throughout America and beyond.

Thousands of long-haired young adults began pilgrimages into Mexico hunting 'shrooms and seeking guidance from God. Many had read magic mushrooms in Wasson's 1957 *Life* magazine article. Soon it was discovered that magic 'shrooms could be found in Texas, west to the Florida Coast, and north to South Carolina.

Eventually, mushroom enthusiasts came to realize that magic mushrooms were not restricted to pasture lands, but also grew abundantly in lawns and gardens in public parks, around homes, and private properties throughout the Pacific Northwest.

Magic mushrooms were found fruiting in lawns and mulched gardens of apartment complexes, office buildings, fire station lawns and mulched garden beds of city jails. 'Shrooms have been harvested from the lawns at McDonald's, Wendy's, Burger King, Jack-in-the-Box, Taco Bell—even the International House of Pancakes.

Psilocybian mushrooms enjoy a wide variety of habitats, including flat-bottomed valleys, gentle slopes or small hills situated along cattle trails in woods and mountainous regions. Some *Psilocybe* species are common in manured fields, rice paddies, meadows and well-fertilized lawns.

Ron Piper.

Timothy Leary and John W. Allen meet up in 1994 at Gathering of the Minds Symposium.

Psilocybe species grow in fertile manured soil with sphagnum moss, moss along streams

John W, Allen as "The Lunatic is in the Grass" admiring *Psilocybe stuntzii* in a lawn in Tumwater, Washington.

Jochen Gartz

and river banks, dead tree trunks, and even branches. They grow on twigs and stems in deciduous woods, and in wood chip mulch layered in gardens surrounding public buildings.

After locating a good field or local neighborhood when hunting mushrooms, one might find more than one species of magic mushrooms in that field or lawn. Word of mouth communication by fellow mycophiles is another source for reliable information on mushroom locations. I have ridden on a city bus, looked out the window and seen people picking mushrooms.

An avid mushroom hunter requires certain equipment to get through a day of picking. When hunting for wild mushrooms, one needs basic mushroom hunting supplies. Such equipment includes paper bags, weaved baskets, and cardboard carton boxes. Opened plastic flat containers are preferred by most 'shroom hunters because they are ideal for preserving the quality of freshly harvested mushrooms.

Prakitsin Sihanonth

Stuck in a heap of compost.

Never place freshly picked mushrooms into plastic bags, baggies, or metal containers. Always keep bags, cardboard boxes and plastic containers opened. Rain clothes might be necessary because mushrooms grow rapidly during and after a rainfall.

The best time to pick fresh mushrooms is a few days after the rain has stopped. Mushrooms dry naturally in the sun a few days after a rainfall but are better preserved when picked while still wet. This is true for mushroom species that belong to the genus *Copelandia* and *Panaeolus*, which have a weaker physiological makeup than those in the genus *Psilocybe* and consequently tend to be hard to transport because they tend to fall apart after collected, with stems or caps breaking into several splinters if dropped.

Angry Shroom

Panaeolus cinctulus in composting hay.

In Florida and the Pacific Northwest, both *Copelandia* and *Panaeolus* species are common in rotted haystacks. Even *Psilocybe cubensis* may be found in composting hay where horse manure is piled. For safety, be sure to park vehicles far away from where one might be picking mushrooms. Security of 'shroomers will be insured by not parking next to a picking location that

Harvesting a small collection of *Copelandia* species from composted straw and manure in rocky soil.

Prakitsin Sihanonth

could attract the attention of the farmer or law enforcement officials, from noticing one on private property. If caught on private property, 'shroomers can be hassled and even charged with trespassing. Avoid this. Always ask permission to go onto private property. Show respect and the owner might allow a perspective mushroom enthusiast to venture forth out onto his property for a few hours.

Some farmers charge mushroom pickers a small fee for collecting mushrooms on their land. Still today, one might befriend farmers who may allow mushroom hunting on their land.

Do not bring dogs into the field. Do not litter the land. Never leave a gate open or unlocked. These are but a few of the many reasons why farmers do not want strangers on their property.

Never encourage cattle to approach you along a barbed-wired fence as the girl in the photo did. Being friendly to the cow who might wish to lick the salt from the palm of one's hand is not good for the cattle. Cows will attempt to poke their heads over or through the wire to check you out and can rip their throats on the barbs, which is another reason farmers do not like 'shroomers in their fields.

A word of caution: Be extremely careful when harvesting fresh mushrooms in the South and Southeastern United States. In 1976, two Tennessee men were shot in the back of the head and killed by a Florida Policeman who caught them trespassing in a field of wild psilocybin mushrooms outside Parkland, Florida. What is sad about this is that the two men were hand-cuffed together at the time of their death.

In 1979, I met a long-haired, long-bearded maniacal local hippie known as "Mushroom Dan" who was a self-described expert in wild edible plants in the forests of Florida. He informed me that the officer was charged with involuntary manslaughter and sentenced to 8-years in prison However, I have seen no report to verify this account of the officer's sentence.

Some farmers use rock salt in shotguns to "teach" 'shroomers that they should not trespass on their properties. Under Florida law, *Psilocybe cubensis* is not illegal to pick or possess, but the alkaloids *psilocybine* and *psilocine*—the active properties in the mushrooms—are controlled substances and are subject to Federal laws.

When collecting mushrooms in third world countries such as India, Thailand, Cambodia, Indonesia, and Vietnam, there are few fences to keep 'shroomers out because cattle and buffalo wander freely and the mushrooms grow wherever the buffalo roam. In these countries there are no laws prohibiting trespassing. Local peasants, farm-

Girl entices cow to sick head through a barb wired fence.

Chao Samui children hunting dinner—the squirrel, shot with a slingshot—offering a mushroom for sale.

ers, and their children may appear from out of nowhere offering to assist you in the collecting of fresh mushrooms in their fields or they might attempt to sell some to you.

In recent years, the ludible use of the sacred mushrooms had become a fad amongst young adults and college students throughout Mexico. Even in some of the remote mountain villages in the Mexican State of Oaxaca or in Jalisco, Veracruz, one may inquire about the availability of the mushrooms in some of the small local village hamlet market stalls.

Magic mushrooms are still very popular and sought after by Western tourists vacationing or trekking through the jungles of Oaxaca, Colimas, and Jalisco, Mexico often ask local vendors where they might obtain magic mushrooms for an all-night velada? Such sales are still common at Palenque.

The three most common mushrooms offered for sale to tourists around the ancient ruins of Palenque—a popular place to "trip"—are *Psilocybe cubensis, Psilocybe mexicana,* and *Psilocybe caerulescens*. The latter species is referred to locally as the "derrumbe"—landslide mushroom. It is the same species consumed by R. Gordon Wasson, his wife Valentina Pavlovna Wasson and their daughter Masha, along with photographer, Alan Richardson during the summer of 1955 in Oaxaca. Five years later in 1960, Timothy Leary consumed 7 specimens of *Psilocybe caerulescens* while on vacation in Cuernavaca, Mexico. This species is known from Alabama, Mississippi east to Florida and north to South Carolina.

By 1974, I read Timothy Leary's *High Priest,* an autobiography in which Tim described his first mushroom experience after consuming seven fresh, gnarly specimens of *Psilocybe caerulescens*, a species known as *Derrumbes*—an epithet signifying the mushrooms as "landslide" mushrooms.

Although *Psilocybe caerulescens* occurs in several Southeastern States in America, in Oaxaca, Mexico, the species fruits abundantly along landslide areas next to sugar cane fields. They also grow in large colonies along the roadways in and out of the sugar cane fields where mud slides occur. When the summer rains appear, the *Derrumbes* are harvested by the pound and then dried on newspapers laid out in sunny areas to preserve then for later use. Sometimes they are placed on large dried leaves laid over on top of old newspaper.

In Mexico, *Psilocybe caerulescens* is the second most popular species used by Mazatec sorcerers, shamans, curanderas/curanderos, and sabias/sabios—both male and female—when *Psilocybe mexicana*—parajito, little birds, the most popular and

Left: Timothy Learys' 1968 1st hard-covered edition of *High Priest.* Right: Ronin's.1995 paperback.

tranquil of species, is not available for use in ritual-like performed sacred and healing curing ceremonies when Derrumbes are used.

The mushrooms Leary consumed while he and his friends were basking in the noon day sun alongside their swimming pool at a rented villa were obtained by anthropologist Frank Baron. Baron had spent a couple of days wandering a local Mazatec village marketplace asking quietly of the native vendors where he could purchase "sacred" mushrooms.

Unsuccessful in his quiet whispering inquiries, Baron switched to the Mexican word "hongos." Eventually, he succeeded in obtaining a bag of really nasty, gnarly looking mushrooms from an elderly local Indian woman known as 'Crazy' Juana. The cost was but a few pesos plus three days of being one of only a few foreigners in a village where everyone knew what he was seeking.

This first mushroom voyage by Tim and his friends was in the summer of 1960 while they were on hiatus, vacationing in Cuernavaca, Mexico. In *High Priest,* Tim described how he learned about the magic of the mushrooms after reading about them in R. Gordon Wasson's *Life* magazine article.

I, too, read the *Life* article after Dr. Daniel Stuntz of the University of Washington's Mycology Department provided me with several references on the most common *psilocybian* literature. Dr. Stuntz also provided several other references on mushrooms published in journals authored by ethnobotanist Richard Evans Schultes who described the historical use of the mushrooms by Aztec priests and their followers during and after the conquest of Nueva España.

Andrew Weil's published an article in the 1960 issue of *Look* Magazine that reported on the Harvard Drug Scandals resulted in the firing of Timothy Leary and Richard Alpert—Baba Ram Dass. Another fantastic read was a personal bio-assay of a psilocybian mushroom inebriation by Greek scholar Richard Graves that appeared in the *Atlantic Monthly*.

Soon the entire world learned of an alleged mushroom cult that held ritual-like sacred healing and curing ceremonies in the

High Sierra Mazateca range of Oaxaca, Mexico. The personal accounts of mushroom experiences provided the world with the subjective physical and visual effects of the mushrooms that later inspired me to become a 'shroomer.

Trappy76

Ruins at Palenque is a popular place to take sacred fungi.

Two 1960s books worth mentioning are John Lincoln's *One Man In Mexico* and Nat Finklestein's, *Hongi Meester*, a personal account of Nat's all night mushroom *Velada* as published in the Journal *Tomorrow* and republished in *The Psychedelic Review.*

In their own words these authors wrote poetically what they saw and felt while under the influence of the divine mushrooms. Those writings inspired me to realize that the tin-canned hermetically sealed alleged divine mushrooms my wife and I had eaten in Oregon were definitely not real magic mushrooms at all.

A year later, some friends in Portland purchased a can of the same reddish syrupy mushrooms. They too were suspicious about the effects of the canned mushrooms, so had them analyzed for chemical content. That was when we learned that the mushrooms in the can were nothing more than the common grocery store edible species, *Agaricus campestris*. In Europe, similar cans of sealed mushrooms from Asia are still sold today. However, the European canned phony magic mushrooms were found to be *Shitake* species. And that now brings me to sharing with all, a true tale of the 'shrooms and how I began my life long journey into the study of these magnificent objects of desire.

SIX

Valley of the 'Shrooms

My first real mushroom high was launched with one quarter to one third of what would be considered a small dose. It consisted of a total of 24 small to medium-sized specimens of *Psilocybe semilanceata*—liberty caps.

I looked back at this period in my life as a turning point, tho I consider it ironic that I had misidentified the liberty caps as *Psilocybe pelliculosa*, basing my identification from a single photograph mailed to me by famed mycologist Alexander H. Smith of the University of Michigan. Dr. Smith with Rolf Singer published in 1958 the first monograph of the neurotropic *Psilocybe* species from the Pacific Northwest United States and Mexico.

My first mild dosage of 24 "liberty caps" from a pasture in West Eugene, Oregon

What was interesting about the Singer and Smith monograph is that they excluded mentioning the occurrence of *Psilocybe semilanceata* from the Pacific Northwest in their ethnomycological study of the Aztec mushrooms referred to as *teonanácatl* and their relationship to the active *Psilocybe* species in North America.

Years later at a mushroom conference I asked Dr. Smith why he had not noted in his monograph that *Psilocybe semilanceata* was

Oregon farm pastures where the divine "liberty cap" lurks.

wide spread in the Pacific Northwest from Northern California to British Columbia. His reply was that he had observed *Psilocybe semilanceata* in the early 1940s in British Colombia, Canada and in Washington State and decided that since the species was already known and reported from several European countries, including the UK, he felt there was no need to include it in the monograph as it was not pertinent to their 1950s study of the Mexican and North American *Psilocybe* species.

I was fortunate to have a photograph loaned to me a year earlier after inquiring Dr. Smith had any photos of species from the pacific northwest (PNW) that I might be able to use as an aid to identify *Psilocybe* species. Subsequently, I learned that the mushrooms I had harvested in a swampy pasture in Eugene, Oregon were the famed liberty caps—*Psilocybe semilanceata*; yet I thought they were *Psilocybe pelliculosa*, based on my macroscopic comparison of the liberty caps I picked with their look-a-like cousins, *Psilocybe pelliculosa.* In the early 1970s, "Ho-dads" or tree planters of the forests in Oregon called *Psilocybe pelliculosa* "elves stools" and "woodland caps".

Watering *Psilocybe semilanceata.*

On that first day I found 24 fresh medium specimens along a fenced-in swampy pasture area surrounded by clumps of sedge grass in a semi-drier area of pasture lands located at Bertel's Packing Plant next to Eugene, Oregon Fern Ridge Reservoir. I climbed a barbed-wire fence, crossed the railroad tracks next to the Reservoir, and then ventured into a swampy pasture where the cattle roamed through trees with scads of mudpuppies scrambling about mating.

After returning home that evening, I consumed 24 'shrooms while still fresh. I remember gagging a little while munching them down. I felt a slight whistling of the wind echoing in my ears. A mild feeling of euphoria spreading throughout my physique, but I experienced no visuals I'd heard so much about.

On the following day, I discovered a second field in a privately owned farm located east of Eugene, just past Noti. The farm was owned by cattle tender Lester Hale and had been in his family for more than 100 years. There were pastures on both sides of the highway. Those on the left were "'shroom happy'". I knew instantly that this field is where I would find the famed divine liberty caps of Oregon.

Until that day I had scoured Oregon, traveling hundreds of miles, walking past my prize, while looking in manure for *Psilocybe cubensis*. In the early 1970s, the only book available on magic mushrooms was F. C. Ghouled's, *Field Guide to the Psilocybin Mushroom*.

Caleb Brown

Psilocybe pelliculosa

Ghouled intended his book be used to identify a few species of the divine mushrooms found in the southeastern United States; primarily in Florida and Texas. It is ironic that because all the while I was looking in manure for *Psilocybe cubensis*, I was walking right over the very liberty caps I was seeking. Then in the fall of 1974, quite by accident, I learned of Lester Hale's shroom farm and his fields of divine mushrooms, the famed 'liberty cap' species—*Psilocybe semilanceata*—that I thought were *Psilocybe pelliculosa*.

SEVEN

Searching for the Elusive Divine Fungi

I learned of the magic holy land with a ‘shroom hunting companion, Rory Johnson of Elmira, Oregon who had picked me up hitch-hiking. His car got stuck on a muddy logging road so we had to hike down the mountain because we could not get the car out of the ditch where it had slid due to a landslide of mud. Rory and I reached the highway between Crow and Noti and we stuck out our thumbs, looking for a phone to call for help with his vehicle. We were pretty muddy from trying to get the vehicle unstuck up the mountain road.

Soon we were offered a ride after meeting some similar-minded folks in a van loaded with about ten pounds of freshly picked liberty caps. They told us where they had found them, and a few of the people in the van were eating caps and tossing the plucked stems out of the van’s window. They did not know that the stems were also vessels of magic potions not to be tossed out a car window.

Although they offered us both some mushrooms, we declined and informed them that we would like to go discover our own magic. Then as they dropped us off when they reached their destination, the driver said that we should continue down the highway from Walton’s Mountain and soon we would see the farm they had told us about that was just beyond a little country store in a township called Noti.

The driver said that for $10 dollars, the farmer who owned the land was very people friendly and that he would rent us a blue bucket to collect our mushrooms; adding that, in that manner, the farmer could look out from his home and see who was in his field. If he saw pickers with one of his bright blue buckets then he knew they had permission to be on his farm. If not, he would send a ranch hand out to chase those away who did not pay him. If those pickers who had no blue buckets caused problems, the farmer called the Sheriff to send an officer to his farm and charge those who had no blue buckets with trespassing on his property.

Back then in the 1970s, many farmers actually put up signs saying, 'No Trespassing' or 'No Mushroom Picking' while other land owners who grazed cattle rented buckets to pickers and make good money on the weekends. Some farmers made as much as $300 every weekend from 'shroom' pickers.

Additionally, a few trespass busts or tickets occurred with some pickers. An 80-year-old grandma held seven teenagers at bay with a shotgun whom she caught trespassing on her properties. When the County Sheriffs arrived, they arrested *her* for terroristic threatening and let the seven kids go after making them dump their 'shrooms.

Later, through several mushroom workshops and conferences, I learned that the liberty caps grew north from Bandon, Oregon, to Vancouver, British Colombia, along the I-5 corridor and from west of the Cascades east to the Olympic Mountains. They are known to also be common along the West Coast region of Northern California as well.

Jochen Gartz

Picking "liberty caps" in tall grass in an Oregon pasture.

Finally arriving at this farm on that cold November day, my

friend Rory and I had crisscrossed the field for about an hour and picked over 400 mushrooms each. We carefully examined them from cap to stem, colors, sticky pellicles, striate margins, incurved margins, some with a few tads of bluing at the base of a stem and others had white gills; sterile specimens that for some reason or other did not produced any spores.

Although I was still using Alexander H. Smith's single photograph in an attempt to properly identify the mushrooms, at the time I realized that these local high school kids who picked them referred to them as liberty caps. Of course, I did not know the difference between a liberty cap—*Psilocybe semilanceata*—and its look-a-like cousin, *Psilocybe pelliculosa.*

At the time that Rory and I found this farm, I was not aware that there were actually several pamphlets published for identifying the divine magic mushrooms that grew in the Pacific Northwest. Two of the most popular field guides had been written by Leonard Enos and Everett Kardel. Their guides were used for finding liberty caps, and the illustrations and water colored renditions were copied from the journal publications of Drs. Rolf Singer and Alexander H. Smith's 1958 monograph on the genus *Psilocybe* published in the academic journal *Mycologia.*

The primary features of that monograph were the line drawings and illustrations of the known species identified by the authors of several species that occur in the Pacific Northwest. They included generic macroscopic descriptions of local species common to the region. Those sketches were later copied and incorporated by Enos and Kardel who reproduced the sketches in those little booklets sold in local bookstores in Oregon and Washington States.

One of my most memorable daily habits was to hitchhike to Lester Hale's field, bringing a one-gallon waxed milk carton container to put my mushrooms in. Some friends in Eugene had informed me that I

Caleb Brown

Psilocybe semilanceata

could easily hitch a ride out to Lester's farm, a distance of about 16 miles from Eugene. In that mode of transportation, I would arrive and since I had no car, it would save me from any hassle in case a police car drove by and noticed a parked car along the roadside next to the farm.

Because I came and went silently by myself, I never had to worry about being hassled while picking mushrooms. Some days, people driving down the highway would look out into the fields and see me bending over. Sometimes they would even honk their horns and wave to me as they passed by; many with fishing poles sticking outward through their car door windows. I guessed that they going to Florence on a fishing excursion. On a few occasions some stopped, pulled over alongside the road, waving at me to approach them so they could ask me what I was doing. Seems some thought that I was digging earthworms to go fishing; One guy asked me if I had seen any night crawlers while harvesting mushrooms from the field.

At times, cattle can be a problem, especially the bulls. One farmer whose fence I had hopped over into his field on a light rainy day saw me coming. An hour later went I went to leave his field he turned on the electric fence. I was out cold for about twenty minutes. When I awoke from the shock, I got up, quite soaking wet and very cold. I slowly crawled through carefully immediately stuck my thumb out to hitch a ride. The first car driving by pulled over offering me a ride.

I related to the driver what had just happened to me and he grinned, saying, "My dad had a bull. Very stubborn was this bull because he kept getting caught in the barb wired fence. So one day my dad turned on the electricity to the fence on high and waited a few minutes and the bull put his head through a hole in the wire and got zapped at full strength." Then this fella began to laugh. "Shoulda seen the look on that bull's face. It was nothing more than pure shock! He never

Alan Rockefeller

Psilocybe semilanceata

A key to the American Psilocybin Mushroom (1970)

went near the fence again." and I learned that lesson really well.

On a few occasions I entered some pastures where I was actually chased by a small herd of young buck bulls. And I ran. One time a lone Brahman bull had me cornered for almost an hour. Every time I tried to move my position, he stepped forward. Eventually I had to wait about an hour for his ass to get moving away from me so I could get out of the field. So! Beware of male cattle.

In later years, I gave Lester free copies of my book, *Magic Mushrooms of the Pacific Northwest,* which he sold to pickers to earn extra cash. Because I gave him copies of my book, he would allow me to wander freely through his fields at no charge.

After finishing my annual daily picking affair I would hitchhike back to my home in Eugene with the milk carton by my side. By the way, a one-gallon waxed milk carton container holds approximately 1200-1600 fresh liberty caps of various sizes, or approximately one fresh pound by weight. When dried, that fresh pound shrinks down to about one and a half dried ounces.

On one such expedition, a county police car drove by and the officer took a good look at me, noticing that I was carrying a gallon of milk down the highway with my thumb out hitching a ride. I was hoping he would think that I had just come from the country store and was going home. He offered me a ride so I got into his cruiser and headed down the road towards the Noti Market, which, if the office believed my story, would have been in the other direction. However, after a few minutes down the road, he glanced at me with a serious look in his eyes, and looking straight at me he commented. "Been 'shroomin'?"

At first I was a little freaked out at his query and then I admitted that I had indeed been out in the fields. So I confessed to the Sheriff that I had been picking 'shrooms.' He next inquired of me what I was going to do with them. So I told him I wanted to keep them for large parties and I would make a tea out of them for everyone. He seemed pleased at that response and said, "Good! I am really glad you were not going to sell them. I would have had a different attitude if you had told me you were going to sell them."

Interestingly, during the whole decade of the 1970s, most law enforcement spokesmen reported to newspaper journalists that there were no psilocybine mushrooms in the area. They made statements reported in the local newspapers that they had analyzed dozens of pounds and found no illegal substances. One Sheriff in Oregon even claimed, "All you need to do is eat a few of those mushrooms and drink a couple of high-balls and you would get quite a bang."

While collecting these prized possessions, I made a habit of counting 'shrooms and one day I had picked, again by crisscrossing a field or two, more than 6,000 liberty caps. This took close to 7 hours of picking. My usual three times a week of pickings were from 1200 to 1600 mushrooms for each trip to the fields.

I conversed with the mushrooms while collecting them in the field, asking them, "Where is your brother, your cousin, your uncle. I am here for you." I thanked them for being there in that humble field for me and wished them well, and hoped that a new family would be ready for me to come and pick in a few more days.

This experience of my first discovery of a large field with thousands of mushrooms was a delight. Over the years my thanking the four winds and the four corners of the universe for their help in bringing me to the mushrooms eventually paid off big time. I do thank them for being there for me and for all of you who seek to enlighten and improve certain aspects of your life when you form a symbiotic relationship with those who hunt and learn from their divine magic.

Magic Mushrooms (1975)

EIGHT

BECOMING ONE WITH THE DIVINE MUSHROOM

After returning home to my wife and son with my bag of 400 fresh liberty caps, we laid them out single file on a newspaper to dry them. We decided to eat some of these mushrooms later in the evening after putting our son to bed.

I suggested that since I had eaten only 24 specimens the night before and had had experienced only a partial feeling of the desired effects of the mushrooms. I felt that the small amount only left me with an uneasy edge what an altered state of consciousness on mushrooms should be. So we decided to consume about forty fresh mushrooms each.

Freshly harvested liberty caps are good specimens for a bioassay.

The mushrooms were somewhat taller in height than the 24 medium liberty caps I had consumed the night before. By weight, this dose of 40 fresh mushrooms would have been the equivalent of one third to one half of a fresh ounce. Today that one fresh ounce would be the equivalent of two to three fresh doses for a psychonauts first experience. However, my wife was insistent that 40 might not be enough, so she suggested we take 60 mushrooms each. Wishing to appease her for the moment, I whole-heartedly agreed with her, and counted out one hundred twenty mushrooms.

The Emerald Princess: Moon Goddess of the 'Shrooms

The high from that many mushrooms turned out to be well over a fresh ounce of liberty caps. It was equal to that of a Mazatec ceremonial dose, producing massive waves of visuals that also pushed our physical euphoria to the max! But the symbiosis of body, the mushrooms and the music we were grooving on was similar to the rapture of cosmic consciousness beyond any realm I have ever experienced or gone to in my entire life.

We consumed the mushrooms, washing them down with chocolate milk. My wife complained that the mushrooms tasted like grass and were nasty, but she consumed them as if they were string beans. It took about 10 to 15 minutes for us to consume them all. I soon wondered if 60 mushrooms might be just a tad too many to eat, and we certainly had no idea of what we were both about to experience.

I watched her gobble down more of her liberty caps, still moaning about the foul and putrid, somewhat acrid bitter taste of the fungi. I realized that someone should always be in control of a trip when taking a new hallucinogenic substance for the first time.

Like an LSD guru or a trip-guide, I remembered that when partaking of a powerful hallucinogenic drug, someone should always be there to help and guide in case of a bad trip. Because this would be a new experience for the both of us, I decided that when my wife was not looking, I would put ten of my mushrooms back into the bag. When I finished consuming my dose, I took care to properly attend to the many fresh 'shrooms I had laid to dry on the top of the stove and in the shelves above the warm stove with the door open for air.

Terence McKenna believed the fresh plant experience was much more powerful than the synthetic experience—having never had the pleasure of tasting the actual synthetic alkaloid psilocine. I thought back to the capsule of alleged psilocine I bought in the early 1970s and was told that I could smoke the powder. But nothing happened when I did. The capsules probably contained LSD, which was common during that decade. The come-on effects of this first real 'shroom high of the large dosage my wife and I experienced was very fast and made us a little nervous at first.

I had read in the writings of the Wasson's that according to Mazatec methods, the mushrooms must be consumed slowly over a 15-20 minute time period. This allows the commencement of the active effects of the tryptamines alkaloid ingredients to take hold of you and gradually build up in your system so as not

Images of on-coming waves of color hit us like "Big, Badda, Badda, Boom."

to shock your CNS. Sometimes, when consuming sacred mushrooms too fast, it causes both your mental and physical mindset to overcome your psyche and spiral your experience out of control.

The mental and physical come-on is quick and swift as the mushrooms enter into your temple of mind and body. When consuming the mushrooms all at once such as in a soup, tea, milkshake or mushroom smoothie, the come-on can be compared to the launching of an Apollo rocket during its initial lift-off: Very fast, very intense, and in less than ten minutes the effect began. This effect is also somewhat similar in effect to a severe shock to the Central Nervous System, causing a mushroom consumer to become impregnated into a temporary state of schizophrenia and most assuredly, many instantly inherit a slight dysphoric reaction to the fast come-on. Some imagine they are dying. There may be a lot of confusion and disorientation during the first half hour and the lift-off eventually settles into a quiet tranquil orbit.

About 15 minutes after my wife ingested her 60 mushrooms; she slowly came to me, saying she wanted to get undressed and go lie down on the bed for a few minutes because she was feeling intensely strange. She said felt a little nauseous and appeared to be quite uncoordinated in her movements. I watched her walk softly to the bedroom. She seemed to be gliding and floating across the room, in harmony. It reminded me of Gary Oldman as Dracula in the film where he meets young Jonathan and Dracula floats across the floor of his stone cold castle.

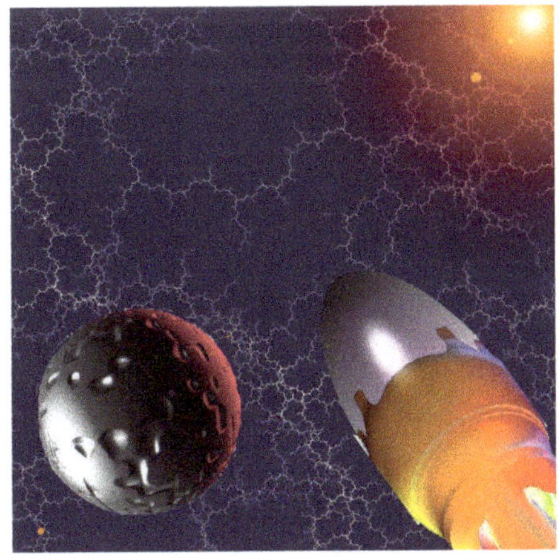

Visuals came in waves and ripples, like a rocket taking off from the Earth to The Moon.

There I sat, all alone in my living room with the TV on wondering if I wanted to watch the movie, "Sounder" or the "Bob Hope" Thanksgiving Special. Before long I, too, felt a bit of queasiness in my gut. After a few more

I took off, flying higher than ever before.

minutes, I heard a voice in the distance calling me from afar. I realized that I had heard my name and amazingly I saw what I had just heard appearing in brilliant colors, vividly floating out to me from inside the bedroom doorway.

The sound seemed as if it was resonating from very far away—kind of like a whispering echo that reverberated in glowing wisps of neon soft colored hues. Instant, I was in awe as I perceived the majestic appearance and wonder of the brilliantly colored molecules of sound that spilled out towards me from across the room, spelling a projected verbal message that only I could hear. It came from somewhere beyond the norms of human consciousness, from an unknown level of intelligence that my cognitive reasoning could never fully interpret. I remember Terence McKenna who spoke of the acuity of vision in monkeys who ate mushrooms and then were able to find new sources of food because their vision had improved while under the influence of the mushrooms.

The feeling of flying is one of the attributes of an entheogenic experience.

The wall was a visual delight, displaying unusually brilliant kaleidoscopic traces of colors zipping about throughout the room.

How could I comprehend that I had just received an incoming call, maybe from another dimensional plane of existence that occurred within the confines of my space producing just a few minute particles of sound. After a few seconds, I realized that my wife was calling me from out of the darkened bedroom. "John?" Again a quiet whisper sounded across the space of our apartment. "John, come here right now. You are not going to believe this." Her whispers reminded me of echoed reverberations bouncing off the earth to the moon and back to our apartment. I arose and walked the long green mile, a distance of about ten feet, like a lost wanderer, a voyager who was about to take his first step into the darkened void of the infinite bedroom.

The on coming waves and ripples of vibrating colors continued to unfold the very fabric of time and space, yet remained stationary as they traveled through uncharted memories.

And then the 'shrooms touched our souls and like a rocket we were transported to another time and place not of this earth. It was then that I noticed there were Escher-like butterfly, caterpillar, and lizard visuals bouncing on and off my walls in kaleidoscopic movements, leaving traces of colors and trails of neon lighting such as I had never seen before. There were grids, embroidered with luminescent lines of colors and neon-like optics bouncing back and forth across the room. They came in waves and ripples. I could feel their colors and hear their silence.

Like echoes and reverberations waves continued their untold tale of time and space.

My body reverberated with their rhythms. They moved in rhythm to the soft music my wife had turned on when she entered the room minutes before I arrived. As I listen, each breath I took became a concerto of longevity. With each breath my flesh quivered in instant rapture with the colors of sound that controlled every mood and thought created for me.

I remember this experience more than any I ever had before that moment. In fact, I remember that night and that moment as if it had happened only yesterday. And I will remember that moment until the day I die and go to mushroom heaven. I thought to myself that, “If I were to die now, then I would want someone to cremate me, roll me into a joint and smoke me so they could gain all the knowledge of my life.

I lay down next to my wife, then asked her to sit up in front of me. As she sat up facing directly towards me, we noticed that we were now both completely naked—not really comprehending how we came to be of purity in the eyes of our creator. As we looked into each other’s eyes in the dark of the room, we could see clearly into one another’s eye, while only a dim light from the living room let us see one another as we were. Everything we ever knew was gone. Flash upon flash hit us with the full thrusting power of a rocket lifting off. We could not think of anything except to touch one another with our eyes and our fingers and we wandered and held together our soul like we never knew we had a soul before this moment. We were again catapulted into a time warp where we could see our aura's surrounding us from the anti-gravity of time and space. We could see we were brightly glowing, bathed in vibrant soft neon colors that pulsed and throbbed to every beat emanating from our hearts and our souls.

I vividly recall the most outrageous colored geometrical and geodesic kaleidoscopic patterns I had ever seen. I looked at them on my hand and I was able to distinguish that they were coming from the 'shrooms. I was not going crazy. They reminded me of Escher Prints, impossible in reality but real in my state of altered consciousness. I continued to observe the continuing patterns of moving butterflies, flowers, and lizards—mud-puppies, wood-living and ground-loving brownish-reddish salamanders.

The salamander's or mud-puppies were the same as those I'd observed in the somewhat swampy-wooded areas along West 11th street near the Fern Ridge Reservoir and out Bartel's Meatpacking Plant. They were the same little fellows I observed on my way cross the railroad tracks and through the wooded area to the swampy pastures of the back lands of Bartel's Meat Packing Plant.

All the Escher-like mud puppies I saw immersing with one another on my wall in vivid color were sending me transmissions from the outskirts of Eugene where I first found my 24 'shrooms the day before. I could feel that the spirits of these living visual entities were looking at me, They were evolving by contracting and expanding to and fro, and coming towards me yet moving backwards all in rhythm to a vivid lined-

Colors just kept on coming and coming like the pulsating echo of my heart, exploding inside of my soul.

We were going up, up, and away to the stars and crescent moons of time gone by and yet to come.

grid, while the sound of Grace Slick singing the theme song from her Manhole album started to get hot and when Grace sang, her words echoed in tune to our movements. I was learning the acuity of and cognitive purposes of my senses now enhanced by the mushrooms I had eaten.

As I lay next to my wife and when she asked me to hold her and touch her, I reached over to her chest and cupped my hand onto her breast. Approaching her breast with the precision of a 747, I made a landing on a runway strip with the accuracy of a perfect alignment, I realized that this landing strip I flew down to where my wife's nude sensual body. I felt the crevice between her breasts. I felt her heartbeat flow from where my hand cupped her breast and my fingers tweaked her nipple and a euphoric sensation followed to my hand from her breast, onto my hand and up my arm until it reached my heart. I became so psilophoric that my senses were overloading with euphoria.

Her breast, like a marshmallow, felt so soft as if it were her melting into my hand. It felt as if my hand had reached inside, deep into her heart, and she transposed and then transported to me, words that only I could hear. Then as the colors of her words flashed directly into my eyes, that new sensation only further fueled the music of her soul.

Those who have experienced this Neotantric form of sexuality know of what I speak; yet it is hard to explain the sexuality that came from that single touch. That touch caused her to experience nothing but multiple orgasms from the moment I touched her breast, and continued for the next three to four hours of our making love. This was a true psilocybian neotantric sexual experience of the third kind. Pure energy of the mind and body so that we now enjoyed a new form of pleasure—a result brought on through the aphrodisiac effects of the mushrooms interacting in a symbiotic partnership upon our neurotransmitters and their relation to *psilocybine* and *psilocine* as it echoed within our very souls.

After this experience I was even more curious about the mushrooms. I visited the University of Oregon's Natural Science Library where I found many articles on magic mushrooms, but unfortunately, their pages had been excised with a razor blade from various pages of journals stacked in the shelves at the school. Some books on magic mushrooms similarly had the photos cut from their pages. This was not a good thing. No one should cut pages from library books. I did not find many papers worth reading and eventually I learned that there were at least 500 known articles on these mushrooms that were

I cupped my hand softly over her breast.

published between the 1950s through 1974 and many were not available to the average person interested in learning about our wonderful friends—our children of the Earth.

It was this single experience that eventually led me into wanting to learn all that I could about the divine mushrooms and that led to me writing my first book, a badly written 24-page field guide with errors in it provided to me by several scholars; many who erred in their identification of several species.

At that time in the mid-1970s, I found that the complete monograph on the genus *Psilocybe* as written by mycologists Rolf Singer of the Field Museum of Natural History in Chicago and Dr. Alexander H. Smith of the University of Michigan had also been completely excised from the pages of the journal *Mycologia.* Thus I spent the last 37-years making the study of these mushrooms my life's work.

During that period, I assimilated into my file cabinets, over 2300 articles on magic mushrooms as well as more than 100 books on the subject of psilocybian fungi, and since that moment of self-discovery, I willingly shared with all, my knowledge to those who shared with me, their interest in learning all that I could offer to them on what I had learned about these mushrooms that made me who I am today.

John with Shasa Shulgin.

PART II

Finding & Identifying 'Shrooms

NINE

Sacred Fungi

Hello mellow fellow 'shroom lovers. The trail of the mushroom is an adventurous trek and many of the various cultures throughout Western civilization have played an important role in spreading the awareness of psilocybian consciousness throughout the world. It has now been more than fifty-seven-years since R. Gordon and Valentina P. Wasson and their team of colleagues announced biblically, the occurrence and use of certain species of entheogenic mushrooms in southern México, reportedly being used in ancient archaic rituals during a sacred 'healing and curing' ceremony referred to as a Velada—an all-night vigil.

During the past thirty-six-years, more than two dozen entheogenic mushroom identification guides and a dozen cultivation manuals have been published for the novice consumer of the sacred fungi. These books show one how to find, identify, harvest, preserve, and cultivate such fungi in one's own home, thus bringing the magic of the mushroom to many where these wondrous fungi do not usually occur.

R. Gordon Wasson

Many of those identification guides provide macroscopic descriptions of entheogenic mushrooms known to occur in North America (including the Pacific Northwest and Southeast United States, as well as Hawaii; México; and Vancouver, British Columbia, Canada).

Several species of entheogenic fungi are also known to occur quite abundantly in the manure of most four-legged ruminants found in both tropical and subtropical islands of both hemispheres. For those mycophiles interested in attaining an altered state of consciousness, the author of this historical tomb has provided amateur mycophiles with up-to-date historical anecdotes of these fungi and presents to the seeker, a proper means of identifying the species described in the book.

The casual use of entheogenic mushrooms for ludible purposes gained public recognition in the early 1960's after Timothy Leary, Richard Alpert and Ralph Metzner initiated their psilocybin research projects at Harvard University. Fear and furor took over as these activities involving members of Harvard's faculty became public knowledge by admitting that some hallucinogenic plants were indeed, as reported by the news media and in the pages of local newspapers, being shared with undergraduate students at the school.

This fact became widely publicized in both the general and popular underground press. For some reason never fully understood, the actual problems within Harvard's elitist hierarchy and their Board of Regents were that students were getting high and the school did not like it. Eventually, Tim Leary was fired for not attending his classes and a month later the school fired Richard Alpert for his refusal to stop giving drugs to students. Years later while reflected back on that period of his life, he acknowledged that he had indeed been fired for providing students with the greatest educational experience of their lives.

By the early 1970s, the ludible use of psilocybin mushrooms slowly became popular in some regions of Palenque in the Mexican State of Chiapas, and Huautla de Jimenéz in the Mexican State of Oaxaca; South America and the Eastern and Pacific Northwest United States and Canada. As early as 1971, Australian surfers became aware of the magical properties of entheogenic mushrooms and in 1972, tourists in Bali and other regions of Indonesia were consuming entheogenic mushrooms in food items such as pizza's, smoothies, soup, and mushroom omelets.

Around the same time in the Hawaiian archipelago, entheogenic mushrooms had already become popular with surfers on Oahu's North Shore. Eventually, foreign tourists from Australia, Bali, and Hawaii learned of the existence of entheogenic mushrooms in the British Isles, Scandinavia and other European countries. Foreign tourists in Indonesia (Java, Sumatra and Bali), South Asia (India and Nepal), and Southeast Asia (Thailand, Cambodia and Vietnam) also learned that entheogenic mushrooms were common in those countries and soon tourists began to seek them out. Furthermore, since the 1990s, magic mushrooms have also become very popular with tourists visiting the Philippine Islands.

Entheogenic mushrooms described in these pages occur in the Pacific Northwest of the United States from Northern California (the Bay Area) to British Columbia, Canada, Mexico, and Hawaii. Rainfall in these regions of our planet provides ideal climatic environments for the abundant growth of several entheogenic species of psilocybian fungi.

The majority of known entheogenic mushroom species in the Pacific Northwest are found mostly in man-made urban environments; occurring in deciduous woods among decayed leaves

Psilocybe cyanescens may resemble *Galerina* species.

and twigs, in mulched garden beds of alder and other mixed hardwoods. Several species also occur in grassy areas such as lawns, meadows, pastures, and in rotted hay and compost heaps at riding stables and racetracks. Magic mushrooms in the Southeastern United States from Florida north to South Carolina and from Florida west to Texas; as in Mexico and Hawaii, occur mostly in the manure of cattle and sometimes horses. A few more potent species occur in woody areas and grassy lawns during cold weather conditions.

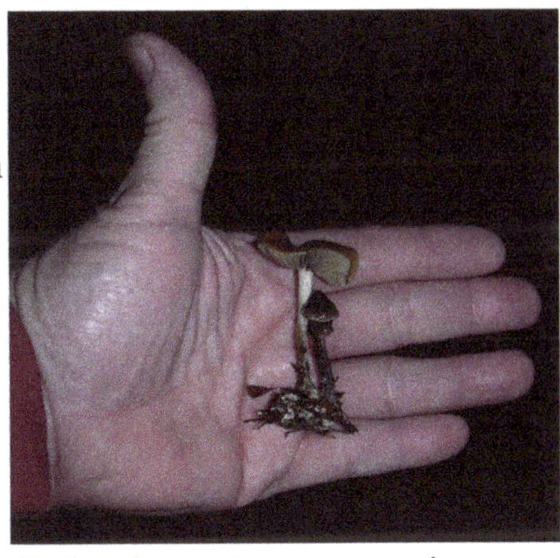

Psilocybe cyanescens and a species of *Mycena* fruiting together.

In this book are featured several of the most common species of psilocybian fungi that are referred to as coprophilous—dung inhabiting—fungi, often occurring in the dung or manured soil of most four-legged ruminants, i.e. cattle, water buffalo, horse, sheep, Indian and Sumatran Rhinos, and elephants.

Species in Mexico share the same habitats as that of the Pacific Northwest and Southeastern USA—in manure, manured soil in pastures and meadows—and sugar cane mulch, sandy soils along streams and river banks, and in deciduous woody debris.

In Hawaii, *Copelandia* species, at least 5-varieties, are common and occur in the manure of cattle and sometimes in manured soil. So far, after 27-years of research in the Hawaiian Islands, no active *Psilocybe* species have been found. Also not so common in Hawaii is *Panaeolus cinctulus*, collected on Maui, Oahu and the Big Island of Hawaii. It was found in fields on Maui fruiting in manure with *Copelandia cyanescens* on Kula Highway up Haleakala Volcano above the 3200 meter marker at the Poli Poli road turnoff up the volcanic mountain.

Many of the etymological names recorded here are from many countries around the world; including, local epithets that may enhance the reader's interest in these fungi. There are also notes provided on methods of preparation, mushroom poisoning, mushroom toxicology, field identification, collecting, and preserving. Additionally a short bibliography of suggested reading materials is provided for those mycophiles interested in broadening their research in this particular field of endeavor.

COMMON NORTH AMERICA SPECIES

The trail of entheogenic mushroom indulgence eventually spread from México to Harvard and then back into the Gulf States and down into Guatemala and South America. The first entheogenic mushroom used as a recreational drug was *Psilocybe cubensis* or *Psilocybe subcubensis* Guzmán. However, both species could be considered as one species since both are macroscopically indistinguishable from one another and can only be separated under a microscope. The difference between the two species is that of the size of their spores. Spores for *Psilocybe cubensis* are larger than those for *Psilocybe subcubensis*. Both species also have a cosmopolitan distribution in the tropic and neotropics of both hemispheres. Furthermore, *Psilocybe cubensis* is known to be grown clandestinely and illicitly out of the sight of law enforcement officials by ludible user's throughout the world in their cellars, cupboards, basements and attics.

In the Pacific Northwest of the United States, the most commonly used entheogenic mushroom is *Psilocybe semilanceata* (Fr.:Sacr.) Kumm. This species is referred to worldwide by users as "liberty caps." This species occurs in pasture lands and lawns—never directly in manure, and is common throughout Great Britain; Scandinavia; Europe; Russia; Once even noted from Africa; North America (Pacific Northwest and Northeastern USA); Australia and New Zealand; Peru, South America; and in Pune, India. The second most popu-

Psilocine Crystal

Steven Peele (FMRC).

Amanita muscaria with an intoxicated snail.

lar species used in the United States is *Psilocybe cyanescens*, a species that is probably the most potent of all by dry weight.

ENGLISH LANGUAGE EPITHETS

In America, as elsewhere throughout the world, entheogenic mushrooms are used ludibly by certain members of society as a tool of recreation and by some as a means of religious enlightenment. Among such users, entheogenic mushrooms are commonly referred to as either 'magic mushrooms' or just plain 'shrooms.'

In 1982, author Peter Stafford was the first to note that the epithet 'magic mushroom' had been inserted into an article authored by R. Gordon Wasson by an editor of *Life* magazine, thus bringing the word to the attention of the public. When the phrase 'magic mushrooms' was first used it was against the wishes of R. Gordon Wasson who never appreciated the insertion of the word 'magic' into his article. Wasson later noted that he had preferred the term 'wondrous' while deploring the now popular and widespread use of the word 'magic' and held reservations about the implications of the use of such a term to describe the visionary effects of the mushrooms in those who consumed them.

Popular Names for Magic Mushrooms

Copelandia species—blue meanies, cone heads, gold caps, dimple tops, witch's tits.

Panaeolus castaneifolius—red caps, subs, subbs, Pan castors, and casters.

Panaeolus subbalteatus (Syn.=P. *cinctulus*)—red caps, subs, subbs, the 'weed' fungus.

Psilocybe allenii—cyanos, cyanofriscosa, cyanofriscana, blue bells.

Psilocybe azurescens—flying saucers, flying saucers, astoryensis, azures, cyclonesi.

Psilocybe baeocystis—blue bells, blue fuckers.

Psilocybe caerulescens—derrumbes, landslide fungi, blue caps.

Psilocybe caerulipes—blue legs, blue foot.

Psilocybe cubensis—gold caps, golden tops, cubes, purple rings, golden teachers.

Psilocybe cyanescens—wavy caps, red saucers, caramel caps.

Psilocybe ovoideocystidiata—blue ringers, blue legs, wavy capped blue ringers.

Psilocybe semilanceata—liberty caps, liberty bells, pixie caps, blue legs, witches tits.

Psilocybe stuntzii—blue ringers, Stuntzii's blue legs, Washington blue veils [once only].

Psilocybe pelliculosa—elves caps, elves stools, woodland caps, fairy caps.

MUSHROOM TOXICOLOGY

In 1957, only seven species of wild mushrooms were identified as entheogens. Today there are over 200 known species. However, because of DNA-ITS studies, along with their results, it appears that there are numerous synonyms used in naming many of

Amanita phalloides (Deadly Toxic).

these 200 reported species. What that implies is that the actual number of species will later be presented to the public when Dr. Gaston Guzman's revised edition of "*The Genus Psilocybe*" is published.

The tryptamine alkaloids in entheogenic mushroom species are psilocybine and/or psilocine. Other tryptamine alkaloids known to occur in psilocybian mushrooms include baeocystine, norbaeocystine, and aeruginascine. These latter three alkaloids produce symptoms and effects similar to psilocybine.

Psilocybian mushrooms also contain other tryptamine derivative compounds that are non-active such as 5-OH-tryptamine, tryptamine and tryptophan. However, many of these tryptamine alkaloids are related to the neurotransmitter serotonine—5-hydroxy-tryptamine.

Psilocybine and psilocine possess a chemical structure very similar to serotonine, a brain neurotransmitter that exerts powerful psychic effects through central sympathetic excitation. Most notable is an alteration of the normal functioning of the brain known as cerebral mycetismus which produces visual effects, auditory hallucinations—synesthesia, and euphoria.

Total intoxication from psilocybian fungi begins within 30-45 minutes after ingestion; lasting up to 6 hours plus when consumed in their fresh or dried form. A slower come-on to the effects may also occur when consumed in food items such as mushroom omelets, stews or pizzas. When the mushrooms are taken in a liquid form, such potions usually are in the form of a cup of tea, or on a bowl of soup, and in the form of a milkshake (mushroom smoothies), when taken thus, the effects commence very fast after ingestion of a liquid potion. This is when the mushrooms are consumed in a short period of time ranging from 5-10 minutes.

The experience will come-on very fast, sometimes presenting a shock to the CNS and that can cause some minor paranoiac panic attacks and mild confusion in those who have consumed the mushrooms in the form of a liquid transport. Some have compared the come on effect to that of a rocket being launched into outer space. However, when taken fresh or dried, take at least 20 to 30 minutes to consume a dosage, then the experience can last from 4-6 hours or longer when consumed over that twenty minute to thirty minute period. The effects from consuming psilocybian fungi vary within each individual and the subjective experience depends entirely on the mood, mental set, and expectations of the taker.

POISONOUS MUSHROOMS

Experimenting with wild mushrooms in any genera can be dangerous even for an avid mushroom hunter. Be sure to thoroughly digest the information in this guide before attempting to journey into a field looking for any of the entheogenic mushroom species described in this book.

Mushrooms come in many different shapes, sizes and colors. There is no guaranteed method outside of a field guide or the knowledge of a trained mycologist to determine what species of mushroom one might come across when searching for magic mushrooms. Many species of poisonous mushrooms sometimes macroscopically resemble and/or mimic their hallucinogenic cousins.

Galerina autumnalis (Deadly Toxic).

Ingestion of some species of toxic non-psychoactive mushrooms will cause the body to flush itself through the bowels and cause severe vomiting. Extreme cramps varying from mild to severe discomfort usually occur after the ingestion of a toxic mushroom species. It is dangerous for a novice mushroom hunter to consume even the minutest part of any wild mushroom without having said mushroom properly identified by someone knowledgeable in the field of mushroom identification.

Amanita phalloides (Deadly Toxic).

The first family of poisonous mushrooms which should be avoided can be found in the genus *Amanita* and they produce a white spore print when laid on top of black construction paper. *Psilocybe* species produce chocolate-brown to purple-brown spore prints, while *Copelandia* and *Panaeolus* species produce black spore prints. *Amanita* species have caps which are scaly. Their stems have a ring near the top and a large bulbous base at the bottom which may or may not resemble an egg (a vulva or a volva). So if one is seeking to harvest any psilocybian species common to their regions in North America, then all those species with white-gills species should be avoided.

The major poisonous species of *Amanita* are usually found in association with pine and birch trees. Most of the *Amanita* species, except for those that are bright crimson red to orange-yellow varieties, contain amatoxins and phalatoxins. They will consume your kidney and liver within 5 to 7 days after ingestion and are usually fatal. The effects and symptoms caused by the deadly toxins in many of the white-spored *Amanita* do not affect ones system until 12-18 hours after consumption.

Similar toxins known to occur in the deadly *Amanita* species also occur in three known species of the genus *Galerina*. They too are also deadly. Some species of *Galerina* are macroscopically similar to several varieties of *Psilocybe* mushrooms. The color of the caps of *Galerina* species vary from chestnut orange to orange rusty-brown. They have a slight ring appearing on their stem. The spore print is of a rusty orangey-brown hue and their habitat includes wood chips, bark mulch and sometimes they may be in lawns. In the Pacific Northwest, some species of

Galerina have been observed fruiting in and around specimens of *Psilocybe allenii, Psilocybe baeocystis, Psilocybe cyanescens, Psilocybe ovoideocystidiata* and *Psilocybe stuntzii.*

While *Amanita muscaria* is toxic in that it is an inebriant of sorts, and several of its variants are also used ludibly by some in today's current yet ever expanding drug subculture. Even deer and snails enjoy_*Amanita* species that are of the 'active kind.'

I wish to stress the importance of learning what species in your neighbor are toxic and deadly so one can separate them from the magic ones that are being sought after. So, I wish to bring to your attention, 3 case studies of mushroom poisonings in young adults and teenagers who mistakenly picked and consumed deadly species thinking they were the same mushrooms they had eaten previously. It is imperative that those who are seriously interested in learning about these sacred fungi that they understand that they should learn all they can so as to not poison themselves or others.

In 1982, two teen-aged boys and a 16-year-old girl became seriously ill after consuming fresh specimens of a species of *Galerina* on Whidbey Island in Washington State. These intrepid youngsters mistook a deadly species of *Galerina*—most likely *Galerina autumnalis*—to be an entheogenic species of *Psilocybe*—more than likely either *Psilocybe stuntzii* or *Psilocybe cyanescens*.

The young girl and her two male companions failed to receive proper medical attention in time because they feared that she and her friends, who also became ill, would be prosecuted for their illegal activities involving the illicit use of the mushrooms. Both boys survived the ordeal, yet both have permanent damage to their kidneys and liver. On Christmas morning, December 25, 1982, the young girl passed away from the toxic species her friends has convinced her to eat along with them, both saying that they had eaten the same species in the past.

Pholiotina filaris (Deadly Toxic).

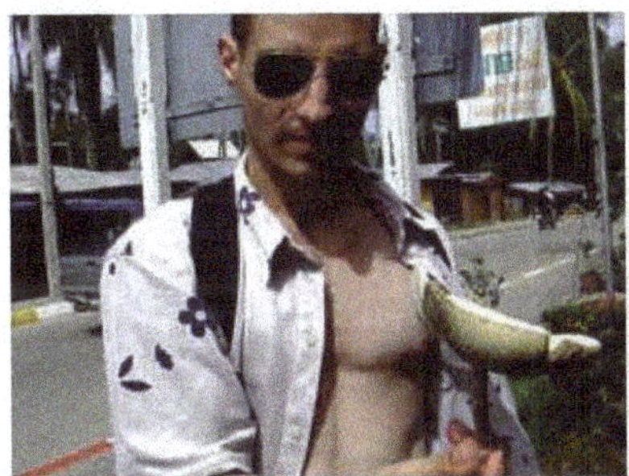

Chlorophyllum molybdites harvested by Grant Trowbridge.

Recently, a newly reported species of *Galerina* from Germany, *Galerina steglichii* Besl., was identified as a psilocybian species and was chemically determined to contain no muscarine, a toxin common in many families of fungi, including *Galerina* species and in many species of *Inocybe*, a genus that also has several psilocybian species that contain no muscarine. *Galerina steglichii* also has orange gills and all species with orange gills (including 7 active species of the orange-gilled genera *Gymnopilus* should be avoided as should the deadly orange-gilled *Pholiotina filaris*. The latter genus of *Pholiotina* has three active psilocybian species in the genus and they should be avoided so as to not confuse them with the deadly varieties. Also, the genus *Conocybe* has recently now had their family name changed to the genus *Pholiotina*.

Another poisonous mushroom which should be avoided is *Chlorophyllum molybdites*. It is commonly referred to as 'green gills' or 'Morgan's Lepiota.' As the nick-name implies, the gills of this species become a light to darkish olive-green in color and that occurs with age. This mushroom is rather large with a scaly cap that resembles a parasol. In Florida, this species has been the cause of much discomfort for many mushroom enthusiasts who accidently mistake this species as *Psilocybe cubensis. Chlorophyllum molybdites* does not grow directly in manure but may be found in manured fields where cattle, horse, sheep, and water buffalo graze. They also occur in lawns in great quantity at times.

Since individual humans have different metabolisms, only a small amount of mushrooms should be ingested during an initial experience. After a 24-72 hour period, one can increase or decrease the amount ingested until a desired dosage feels comfortable. Furthermore, any wild collected mushrooms that a consumer might have suspicions about their identification, may take them to an expert mycologist at any university or college with either a mycology or botany department. Teachers and students alike will be more than willing and quite happy to properly identify any wild mushroom brought to them for identification.

John with Gordon Wasson.

TEN

The Soma Complex

Many species of wild mushrooms contain a substance known as muscarine, a toxin that will cause profuse sweating, severe stomach cramps, nausea and vomiting. It is always a good idea to have in one's possession, a book on edible and poisonous mushrooms when collecting in the wild.

Muscarine is common in active species of the genus *Amanita*, especially in the active inebriating crimson red to yellowish-or-angey varieties. Some psilocybian enthusiasts and aficionados have expressed a desire to consume the various inebriating species of *Amanita,* we suggest that they avoid this family and stick to the fungi they so well love; the chocolate-brown to purplish-brown spore print color of *Psilocybe* species or the jet-black spore print color of *Panaeolus* and *Copelandia* species featured in this book.

Tjakko Stijve

Active European species, *Amanita pantherina* uncommon in North America.

It is believed by many that *Amanita muscaria* was

Amanita muscaria.

the hidden source of the Soma plant described in the 9th and 10th Mandala of the Vedic Hymns in the *Rig Veda*. That species and its close relative, *Amanita pantherina* are used by some young adults and their peers in the Pacific Northwest, in Japan, and in some parts of Europe for ludible inebriations. For a more detailed descriptive history of the cult-like ritual use of *Amanita muscaria* by shamans of several groups of Siberian reindeer herdsman, see Wasson's, *Soma: Divine Mushroom of Immortality.*

Amanita muscaria images featured in this book are from the Pacific Northwestern United States, including Seattle, Washington; Astoria/Hammond, Oregon; Kauai, and the Big Island of Hawaii.

While atropine is used to alleviate the toxic effects of mushroom poisoning when certain species are known by the tending physicians, it should never be used to treat anyone under the influence of either *Amanita muscaria* or *Amanita pantherina.*

The atropine acts as a potentate to ibotenic acid and muscimol and actually increases the level of toxicity in those who have eaten these mushrooms. That in turn makes the already agitated-poisoned person to be vastly higher than when first admitted to ER for treatment.

Amanita muscaria is protected by the Great All Seeing One-Eyed Toad.

PALEO-SIBERIAN

Isolated groups of Finn-Ugrian people, the Ostyak and the Vogul of Western Siberia are known to employ *Amanita muscaria* shamanistically, as do the Chukchee, Koryak and Kamchadal people of Northeastern Siberia. Other reports have indicated that the use of *Amanita muscaria* is not just restricted geographically to western and northern Siberia. Greek Historian Robert Graves and Dr. Richard Evans Schultes of Harvard University have indicated that some Finns and Lapps, in Japan and the Philippines, as well as a small enclave in Afghanistan may use this species shamanistically.

In 1979, R. Gordon Wasson reported that the use of *Amanita muscaria* was common among certain groups of North American Indians--the Ojibway. In two different studies, anthropologist, Dr. Marlene Dobkin de Rios, in her books, *Windmills of the Mind* and *Hallucinogens: Cross Cultural Perspectives*, discusses the strange custom of *Amanita* urine-drinking by the reindeer herdsmen of Siberia. This interesting habit had first been reported by travelers and explorers in Siberia during the late seventeenth and eighteenth century and similar evidence of the urine-drinking was noted by ethnomycologist, R. Gordon Wasson in 1968 as being mentioned in the Vedic scriptures.

Later in 1968, R. Gordon Wasson suggested that some psilocybian mushrooms may have also been employed traditionally in primitive Siberians in archaic-like shamanic culture.

NORTH AMERICAN INDIANS

In North America, *Amanita muscaria* has reportedly been used among two different groups of Native American Indians. In 1979, Dr. Richard Evans Schultes and Dr. Albert Hofmann both mentioned the use *Amanita muscaria* amongst members of the Dogrib Athabascan. In 1978-1979, they reported that female shaman, Keewaydinoquay of the Ojibway used it. R. Gordon Wasson brought to light the fact that the *Amanita muscaria* was also commonly used ceremoniously by the Ojibway of Northern Michigan and Ontario, Canada. The ritual use *Amanita muscaria* by a tribe of North American Native Indians date back almost four-hundred years.

Ethnomycologist, R. Gordon Wasson first brought to light the use of this fungi as being used in ritual ceremonies by Native Americans. In the 1960s, R. Gordon Wasson published a letter from a Jesuit Priest living in Quebec, Canada who wrote to his brother in Paris, also a Jesuit Priest, about the use of *Amanita muscaria* in which those who partook of the fungus would see themselves going to heaven and having sexual intercourse while under the influence of the mushrooms. That letter predated by at

Amanita muscaria.

least 100 years, the first published reference that *Amanita muscaria*, as reported in several 17th century journal publications, was used ceremoniously in Siberian as an inebriant.

This is the only record of a group of North American Indians who have used a mushroom as a sacrament. However, it is also possible that *Amanita muscaria* or its variants may have been used in ritual ceremonies by the Mayans. Active ingredients isolated from this species in 1963 and 1965 revealed that *Amanita muscaria* and several related species contain the compounds, ibotenic acid, muscimol and other active compounds as well as some toxic compounds, primarily muscarine.

ELEVEN

Identifying Psilocybian Mushrooms

To properly identify and key a particular species of fungi to its genus one must first make a spore print. A spore print is one of many paths that teach to what family a particular species of mushroom belongs.

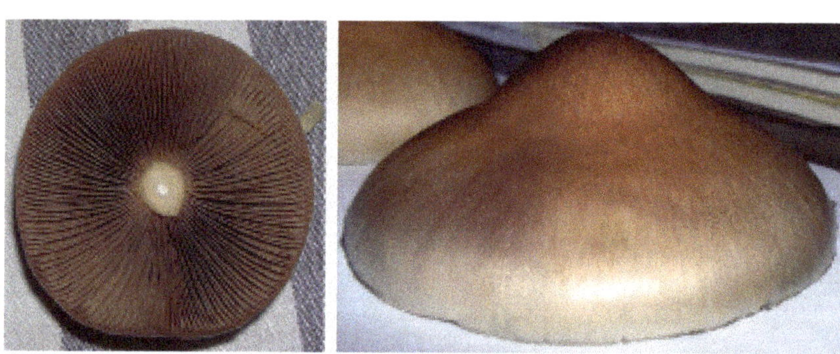

Chocolate brown gills of a Ban Phang Ka, Thailand indoor grow of *Psilocybe cubensis* as it creates a spore print.

Place a mushroom on a white paper with the gills down and cover with a sterile jar. After 20 minutes or more, remove the jar from the paper and lift the mushroom cap from the paper. If the spore print is chocolate to purple brown then the mushroom is probably a Psilocybe.

Psilocybe species have gills and spore colors that vary, ranging in hues from a light chocolate-brown to a very dark violaceous or dark purplish-brown color. The violet colors become a dark purplish-brown and are very uncommon in fields where there are large

A dark violaceous spore deposit on several caps of wild *Psilocybe cubensis.*

herds of grazing four-legged ruminants. These colors can also occur indoors in terrariums through home cultivation.

Sometimes the spore colors present a violaceous hue or even purple-brown spore tone as can be observed after the mushroom's veil breaks open. When the veil has broken the gills under the cap, releasing the spores into the wind, which disburses them onto the caps of the mushrooms in the surrounding vicinity. As the spores settle, they sometimes land on the tops of the surrounding caps in an individual cluster. Most wild specimens will not have those colors and the caps will usually be of a golden tan-straw-yellow color from fresh to dried mushrooms.

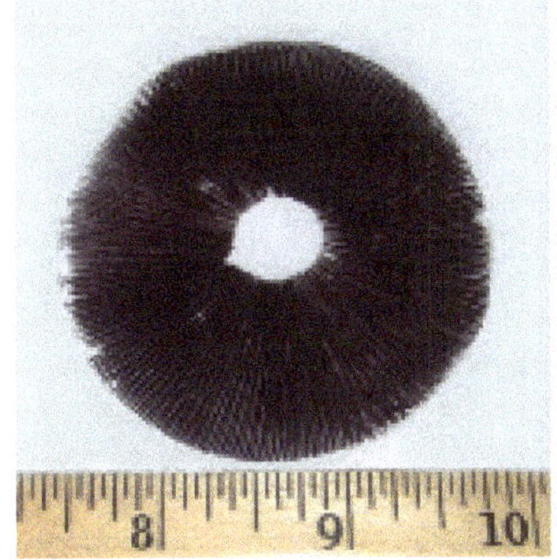

Spore print from a wild Florida strain of *Psilocybe cubensis*. The 2nd image is the new strain results that produced larger specimens.

How to Make a Spore Print

To obtain a good spore print, use scissors or an Exacto blade cleaned with Lysol. Cut the stem off of the mushroom cap and place it face down on a piece of white paper. Next, place a sterile cleaned empty jar over the cap of the mushroom to allow the spores from blowing away.

Not all mushrooms produce spores. Out of every three to five-hundred freshly harvested specimens of *Psilocybe cubensis* one or two specimens may be sterile. The mushrooms in the image are *Psilocybe cubensis* collected in a rice paddie habitat where I had collected several pounds of mushrooms, which are now on deposit at Chulalongkorn University in Bangkok. Shown are the mushrooms as I first gazed upon them early in the morning. In the second frame I hold the two specimens to show the sterility of the find.

Sometimes during a cultivation flush, one might find a single specimen of *Psilocybe cubensis* that is sterile, yet all the other mushrooms have viable prints and reproduce without any contamination or sterility. One might assume that this orange-gilled mushroom was a species of *Gymnopilus* or *Pholiotina*. If you look carefully you can see the blue oxidation of psilocine in the center where I cut the cap from the stem of the mushroom.

With the *Copelandia* and *Panaeolus* species, if their spore prints are jet black, and it is found in manure, and stains blue when damaged, you have found those species you are looking for.

Fresh sterile specimens of *Psilocybe cubensis* harvested to show sterile condition.

A single sterile specimen of *Psilocybe cubensis* grown indoors in a terrarium.

Only two families of black-spored fungi are known to possess the alkaloids psilocine and psilocybine. They include three to eight species of *Copelandia* and two to four species of *Panaeolus,* as well as those that blue are active psilocybian species usually occurring in the dung of most four-legged-ruminants and sometimes in manured soil.

The Bluing Phenomena

Psilocybian mushrooms can be identified by an enzyme which occurs in fungi containing the alkaloids psilocybine and/or psilocine, with an indole nucleus and producing by an oxidative process, a blue pigment.

When the flesh of the stem or cap of a fresh mushroom is bruised or damaged, such as from human handling, wind, insects or falling objects, an enzyme occurs which oxidizes as it comes into contact with air.

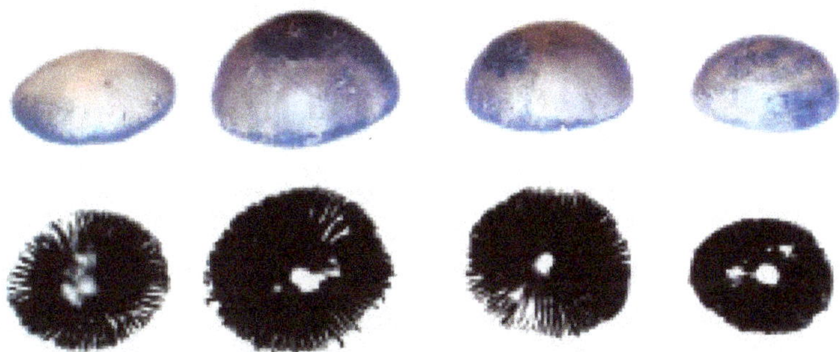

Caps and spore prints of *Copelandia cyanescens.* Oahu, Hawaii.

Natural elemental damage from monsoon winds caused intense bluing to occur in *Copelandia cyanescens.*

Windy and rainy weather may damage a mushrooms cap or stem, or both, causing them to stain blue or blue green when bruised. Many species of psilocybian fungi have stems ranging in color from a pallid yellow white to an off white hue and when damaged the white begins to stain blue.

Cattle walking through open fields while grazing often kick the mushrooms. Some mushroom enthusiast have seen fresh mushrooms dangling from the mouths of cattle chewing them along with alfalfa or other wild grasses in their natural habitats. Such damage will cause a blue oxidation to occur, which is why one sees a mushroom every now that has bluing already in those damaged fresh mushrooms. Bluing will also occur from sunlight or from drying as the mushroom ages, dissolving back into the topsoil where the spores will become mycelia to begin life anew.

Damage may occur with extreme cold weather when frost or snow sets in. Normally, the bluing reaction occurs within 10 to 20 minutes after human handling but may already be noticeable in fungi damaged from natural elements and from bluing with aging.

There are certain chemical applications in psilocybian mushrooms that speed up the bluing reaction. One method involves "metol", a chemical used in photograph-

Bluing in *Psilocybe allenii* from damage stems.

Bluing in an unidentified species of *Psilocybe.*

ic developing, which until recently could be legally purchased from any camera and photographic supply outlet. Metol is currently available online at numerous Internet sites. Mix 1 part Metol with 20 parts water. Place the stem of the suspected mushroom in the "metol" solution and wait for approximately 1/2 hour. If the solution turns blue, then you have actually collected a mushroom containing *psilocybin.*

One day I crawled under some bushes next to a pine tree and I saw beautiful bluing mushrooms. I immediately recognized certain characteristics of the mushrooms and realized they were indeed an unidentified species of *Psilocybe*.

And then that has family with bluing species that are non-edible or actually toxic belong to the genera *Boletus* and have pores

Bluing in the non-active species, *Psilocybe aeruginosa.*

Á choice-edible species that stains blue-green against an orangey background.

and porous bottoms instead of gills. Blue-staining Boletes are toxic and should be avoided.

Blue to blue green pigments also occur naturally in *Psilocybe aeruginosa, Psilocybe carulea, Psilocybe cyanea* and *Inocybe calamistrata*. They are not toxic or edible and possess no active alkaloids. Another species that stains blue to green is the edible species, *Lactarius deliciosus*, commonly referred to as the Saffron milk cap. It is a big meaty orangey-colored mushroom. It is not active and is a choice edible species.

TWELVE

Mushroom Lifecycle

This is not a tale for the squeamish. So sit back, relax, breathe deeply; and let clean air slowly pass through you. If you live in a place where cannabis is legal, then light up a doobie, inhale, and listen carefully to the sound of your vision— A Tale of the 'Shroom.

I admit this presentation on spore disbursal for *Psilocybe* took a long time to figure out how to best present. I must let you know ahead of time that some of the 'shroom images with the worms are from different days and different mushroom caps, which after making a print, I laid aside to dry but the humidity was so horrible that it caused the worms to hatch. So I put together a beautiful stunningly 'Sporetacular' pictorial visual presentation on what exactly occurs in the lifecycle of a mushroom.

Although, this is primarily written for the south and southeast United States and Hawaii, cattle, no matter what breed, provide the manure that certain spores are probably sexually attracted to one another; like flies are to manure heaps. To illustrate my point of evolution of a spore, I will note that in Thailand, there are 65,000,000 water

Oliver of Samui Beach Resort.

Rice Paddies of Ban Hua Thanon, Koh Samui.

Water Buffalo create the manured heaps that promote mushroom propagation.

buffalo, of which approximately 10,000,000 are pink.

About 6,000,000 cows, mostly of the genus *Bos* are composed of Brahman Bulls and dairy cattle. *Bos gaurus, Bos sundaicus*, and *Bos indicus* and other four-legged ruminants also inhabit the region—all producing manure that brings about the fruiting's of several common neurotropic species.

In America there are half a million Brahman Bulls from Texas to Florida. The males are raised for breeding and meat products. They do enjoy the climatic conditions of the deep south and southeastern United States.

The water buffalo and Brahman cattle are the progenitors of several species of magic psilocybian mushrooms known to occur in the manure of these four-legged ruminants or in the manured ground. Among these mushrooms are *Copelandia cyanescens*, covering at least 5 other binomials, and *Psilocybe cubensis*. This study focuses on the evolutionary metamorphosis of *Psilocybe cubensis* from dung to flies to fly eggs to spores to 'shrooms to breed fruit fly larvae up the insides of the stipe and then watch the worms eat the meat of the cap, until the large meaty tissue becomes a gooey glob of black inky slime.

Brahman bull.

The Mazatec speak softly of the appearance each sea-

Cubes with full veil of spore deposits.

son by proclaiming in secrecy to one another "that the little mushroom comes of itself, no one knows whence, like the wind that comes, we know not when or why".

A mushroom pops up in the manure of four-legged ruminants, preferably that of buffalo and cattle-cows, sometimes even fruiting in the manure heaps of horses and elephants. When the mushroom reaches maturity, the cap opens and a veil remnant, as seen in the photo, drops, and so do the spores. I watched my 'shrooms grow. Returning a few hours later, I noticed that while I was away, the veil had dropped and the cap opened wide, releasing millions, if not billions of spores disbursing, immediately flowing into the air and surrounding environment. Imagine, millions of spores disbursing through the air where many drop directly below the mushroom and on to the grassy surrounding earthy habitat. This is the beginning of the lifecycle of the mushroom.

Spores are disbursed in different ways. Falling directly below the caps of the mushrooms, landing on the blades of surrounding wild grasses and other foliage in the region. Or cows eat the mushrooms and the spores are disbursed inside one or more of the cow's four stomachs.

Thai boy with giant cube.

Sometimes the cattle and buffalo poop directly on a place where the spores have been deposited on leaves or the ground. Cattle and birds and other small animals may carry spores from

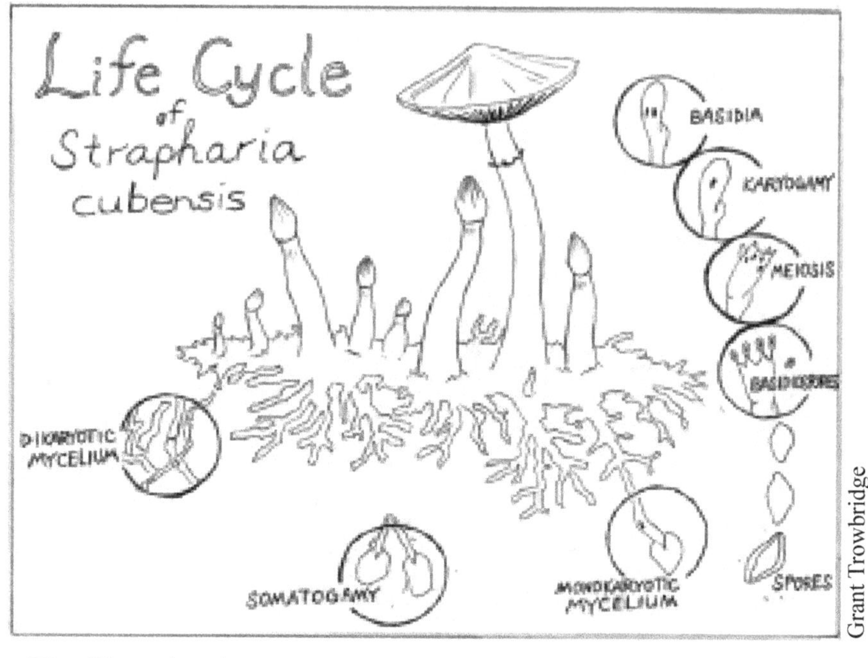

The lifecycle of a mushroom inspired by Terence McKenna.

one location to another when spores are lodged into their hooves or beaks.

In 6 to 8 weeks or so, after the manure has decomposed, new mushrooms began to appear. The sketch illustrates the lifecycle of *Psilocybe cubensis* and this spore disbursal evolutionary process is commonly found in most of the known species of the *Agaricales*.

TALE OF THE 'SHROOMS

On a hot and humid morning in 1987, while vacationing on Koh Samui, an Island in the Gulf of Thailand, I awoke to the sound of a song being sung by a bird, somewhere nearby outside of my window. I could tell by the sound of this warbler that it was telling me to arise and greet the day with a 'shroomy smile.

After getting up and taking a quick shower, I checked on the mushrooms I picked the previous day to see if they had dried overnight while on my nightstand in my bungalow room.

On that wonderful, warm morning, I slowly became aware that the semi-dried mushroom caps I had placed on white paper on my night table seemed to have dozens of tiny holes drilled by a small platoon of mini carpenter ants; and their big brothers, the soldier ants.

It was the "Time of the Ants." They marched in a single-file line from outside my bungalow, up three stairs and straight inside to one leg of my night table, then climbed to the top of the table where the mushrooms lay. All night long the ants chewed and gnawed their way into the heart and meat of my harvested children.

I had never before encountered this problem when drying mushrooms or making spore prints. I've often collected mushrooms from lawns and mulched garden beds and placed them on paper in cardboard boxes to dry, or make prints, and every now and then I might see a mini-slug eating on a fresh cap or a creepy crawling insect come out of the gill-plates of a cap, then scatter crazily around the newspaper looking for another cap in which to hide.

"Why me?" I wondered. How had I drawn the ants into my space. Instead of the beautiful mushrooms being properly preserved for creating spore prints and other specimens for herbarium deposits, I was staring at a hundred or more ants running in circles around the drying mushrooms. Yes indeed, the ants appeared to be extremely confused, and of course they were because they were all stoned. Why else would they be running around in circles when they are usually so organized, marching single file?

You can see the little tiny holes drilled by the ever-clever hungry ants. Ants seem to love entheogenic 'shrooms and my beautiful 'shrooms were the kind of 'shrooms that Island Carpenter ants of Koh Samui love to nibble on.

The picture shows the caps in which the ants drilled holes in while feasting on the magic of the 'shrooms.

Oliver of Samui Beach Resort

A birdie at my window sings softly.

Ants infested, then drilled holes into 'shrooms drying overnight.

I found it fascinating that the onslaught of the ant army had created a one-way single-lane super roadway from the floor that allowed them to climb up the leg of the table to where the mushrooms were drying overnight. They probably had actually smelled these mushrooms from their mound. However, there was not a single line of ants climbing back down the table leg to the floor and out the door.

Many ants were still clinging and dangling along the table's edge, peeping directly over the table's edge—while stoned. They were definitely afraid of the height as the floor must have appeared to the stoned ants as being a long, long way down.

I pointed the table fan at them and they scattering off the table. I enjoyed watching them being thrown and tossed around across the table top while some fell overboard, probably screaming although I could not hear any sound emanating from their tiny mouths. Others held on tightly to their 'shroom meal, on as if their very lives depended on it.

When I turned off the fan, the ants regrouped. Dozens of little holes were drilled into the 'shrooms where the ants had been munching. They were probably preparing a war dance as they continued to chew away on the meat of the caps—eating and tripping out on the mushrooms. That was my first lesson in drying *Psilocybe cubensis* collected from manure.

I had had other critter problems in hot third-world countries while trying to preserve my specimens. On my first visit to Koh Samui, giant cockroaches—palmettos—got into my collections of drying fungi. Huge giant-sized big water bug kind of cockroaches chewed gaping chunks from the fresh mushrooms with their gnarly skeletal cockroach teeth.

“My God” I exclaimed when I realized that the roaches were stoned out of their skeletal framed brains just as the ants had been the night before. I immediately sprayed some Lysol into the drawer, waited 15 minutes, then put the ‘shrooms onto white paper into a dresser drawer hoping to keep the big roaches away and produce some good cube prints.

In my next attempt to properly dry more cubes, I put sheets of a local Thai newspaper on top of my mosquito net. Back then most bungalows at the resorts had open aired windows and no screens, so mosquito nets were a necessity to not be bitten on all night long. At the time, the top of the net above my head seemed like a good place to try to dry my mushrooms without the interference of critters invading the harvest and chewing big gaping holes into the caps as they ate them. What a trip for an insect. I wondered what was going on in their little brains while they were inebriated.

I awoke in the middle of the night upon hearing a strange gnarly gnawing sound emanating from the newspaper on top of my mosquito net, which was tiered by rows of drying mushroom caps. I got up and flipped on the light run by a weak generator, so it flickered on and off giving the room an eerie glow of solace. I was listening to the hum of soundless reverberations and the clicking of tiny teeth.

Psilocybe cubensis cap with hole chewed by cockroach.

There, at the edge of the mosquito net, was a large friggin rat dangling and hanging over the edge of the net by grasping the netted fibers with his clenched paws. It was holding on to the edge of the net in fear for his dear meager life; and like the ants and the cockroach of the previous two nights, he too was obviously stoned out of his gourd.

Apparently the rat had a problem in judging the distance from atop the mosquito net to the floor. He appeared to be judging such distance by the way he looked down. It was as if it was wondering if it could leap to the far, far away floor. I imagined he was having a very bad trip and wanted to get away from the big human monster looking at him.

Actually I was looking deep into his frightened twitching darkened eyes. It almost looked as if he was saying "what the frick is going on here?" That's a story for another day.
This was the third evening in a row of my trying to properly dry the mushrooms I collected. When the temperature hits 115 degrees plus intense humidity, the creatures that go bump in the night ate my decomposing mushrooms, which had become soggy, melting into a glob of purple-black dark goo.

Cows and water buffalo commonly consume cubes and copes in their shaded grassy grazing areas of the rice paddie fields, along with other species of mushrooms. When they chew on a mouthful of fresh 'shrooms growing in a large chunk of grass they most assuredly experience an alteration of their consciousness while under the influence of the 'shrooms they consume.

John W. Allen.

THIRTEEN

Spore Dispersal

Spore dispersal is a mighty thing, like a giant orgasm in the air of dried spores blowing in the wind as if Dylan himself saw and knew what I was thinking. The majority of ‘shrooms that grow in dung actually grow from spores deposited on blades of grass or from being inside the stomachs of four-legged ruminants. The spores make their way into their stomachs from animals eating the grasses where spores have been deposited or from eating fresh mushrooms with spores in them. Where spores are deposited reminded me again of the Dylan song that something was ‘blowing in the wind.

Here is that blade of grass with black spore deposits from freshly harvested specimens of *Copelandia cyanescens* that I picked for research. I put the blade of grass inside a petri dish. There were many blades in the grass with *Copelandia* spore deposits on them and there they will remain until some cattle or water buffalo come along and either shit on it or eat the grass with the spores that are deposited on the blades of grass.

Jet black spores of a species of Copelandia deposited on grass.

Observe the large capped specimen of *Psilocybe cubensis* on the next page with spore deposits all over the top of the cap. You can

Purple chocolate brown spore deposit on *Psilocybe cubensis,* outline of blades of grass.

see the area where I removed a blade of grass from the top of the mushroom to photograph the color of the spore deposit on the caps topside to show how a blade of glass above the mushroom can also have spore deposits on the cap.

The next thing you will learn is about how the mighty buffalo —kwai—comes along or the lowly cow—wua—happens by and deposits some of that fodder he was chewing on the day before onto the spores deposited on those mighty blades of grass, and after he drops that fresh turd of dung, flies come along and lay their eggs in the fresh manure so their little unborn larvae can feast in a manner befitting their station in life and their perspective position and stature in their environmental society of the dung of four-legged ruminants.

These flies were many on the pie until I lay down next to their breeding factory and watched while they scattered off in different directions away from me. Eventually they returned after I laid still for a while next to their heaven. They were wall to wall like a carpet in a living room, all of them in harmony laying their eggs together as if a flock of church members were singing a hymn on a Sunday morning in the pews of a local church.

Aha, I thought, not all of them are afraid of me. Many stayed as the next images show the flies depositing their eggs into the heaps of dung. Of course, the image only shows about one-fifth the amount of flies that were laying eggs before I came upon their breeding ground and disrupted their orgasmic egg-laying nest.

Nothing more exciting than lying down with one's face staring directly into a large buffalo turd inches away. The problem was that fire ants and carpenter ants were eating my neck, ear and legs. Then, like in Cambodia, I was attacked by a giant spider crawling up my neck.

That actually happened in West Seattle when I was harvesting a small colony of *Psilocybe cyanescens* that were hiding from me under some Rhododendrons in Lincoln Park. I crawled under the bushes to collect 'shrooms and accidentally put my face directly onto a spider web with one of those giant Banana-looking spiders. I screamed and smashed him and smeared his body across my cheek, screaming until the house owner came out to see what the noise was about. It was creepy as hell. But then, that is another tale to be told at another time and place.

The egg-laying flies wall to wall on the dung heap was a more welcomed sight. Maybe I should have laid there for a while so that all the flies would have returned to Manure Hill in time for me to take their picture and record it into the history books on the evolutionary process of fungi development in which I was partaking.

Eventually, after spores disburse around any given area onto blades of grass or directly into the foliage, the mycelium will format under the manure like in the photo on the next page. There were matted areas of mycelia growing along the bottom outer edges of the mostly dried decomposed manure. There were several baby specimens of *Copelandia cyanescens* pinners fruiting under the manure and reaching over to pop out from the outer edge of the manure. It seems

Flies laying eggs in Brahman bull manure.

Pinners of *Copelandia cyanescens* fruiting where spores fell on manure.

that the worms love to feed on the meat in the stems of the mushrooms, so once they are picked, the worms really eat the caps as the biological death of the shroom occurs and deterioration sets in.

The image below show what happens after dung fell on the several blades of grass lying where 'shrooms had previously grown and died. After several weeks after the manure decomposes, then and only then does the mycelium spread under the pile of the manure as small pinners began to appear.

Sometimes cattle will drop manure heaps on areas where spores had been previously deposited. Four to six weeks after fresh grass appears, the mushrooms will then grow well in those manured areas; sprouting upwards towards the sky. Below is an image of one manure heap with rhizomorphic strands of mycelia where *Psilocybe cubensis* will soon fruit.

As previously noted, *Psilocybe cubensis* and certain species of *Panaeolus/Copelandia* generally produce mycelium that grows under the manure and when the time is ripe the mushrooms appear and grow.

Decomposing manure and rhizomorphic strands of mycelium.

After a few hours of picking, I transport my harvest back to my place of residence to make spore prints. It helps to dry the mushrooms in the extreme heat. As the humidity changes, the eggs inside the cubes stems hatch. Since the stems of many species of fungi are hollow, as is the case with *Psilocybe cubensis,* it is like the tunnel where the light at the end of the is in tune to receive the offerings of the fruit fly larvae as they proceed

Rotting *Psilocybe cubensis* with worms inside.

to make their way up the inside of the stem to the soft cap that is rotting. As the little worms ate the cap, they begin to shit where they are hatching. The smell brought more babies up the stem to join in the festivities going on within the new world worm community.

If the mushroom cap is overloaded with too much water it will harden to create a spore print in the confines of a bungalow resort setting. If the cap is fresh, then one can obtain a beautiful perfect spore print, one that may later be used to help further propagate the species. However, if it is hot and there is no airflow and the humidity is high, then the worms will eat the cap meat from the inside out.

Above is an overturned cap of a lighter brown, with a few worms worming their way out of the center where I cut it with a scissor. I could feel the softness in the cap in the morning as I lifted the cap from the paper when attempting to get a print. I felt that the cap getting soft and somewhat soggy. It was so soft that the tiny worms soon started to perform their "dance of the seven veils" as they wormed their way to ecstasy via the *ananda* of the 'shrooms.

The three caps in the photos are very healthy solid meaty mushrooms and therefore should be ripe enough to produce good quality spore prints. However, the worms hatched due to a high temperature and bad air-flow. These caps ended up becoming small black gobs of goo and the meat of the mushroom caps were, at the moment this photo was taken, being consumed by the fly larvae whom now were having one hell of a tripping party going on inside these caps.

The three caps that deteriorated from lack of airflow and stoned out worms eating them.

FOURTEEN

Copelandia bresadola

Copelandia species are dung-inhabiting mushrooms, often appearing in the manure of four-legged ruminants, like water buffalo, cattle, sheep, horse, elephant, rhino, and are common in the tropics and neotropics of both hemispheres. They are known to occur in aged powdered manure piles that are layered in habitats where the manure is processed by local cattle-farmers to be used as garden fertilizers sold at local markets in tropic and subtropical climates, including the Southeastern United States.

Some *Copelandia* species occur in well-fertilized new sodded or seeded lawns or those that have perpetual lawn care service. When found in newly sodded grassy lawn habitats, the species usually only fruit once or twice after their first appearance and rarely ever return after the nitrogen and phosphates in the soil are consumed by the vast mycelial network that feeds off nutrients in fertilizers that have exhausted their purpose.

Bluing in *Copelandia cyanescens* from natural elemental weather damage.

Copelandia species tend to blue quite intensely and almost immediately when damaged from human handling or from natural elements such as weather, wind, and rain. Sometimes the bluing occurs after cattle or other animals kick the growing fungi with their hooves while passing by a colony inhabiting a dung heap. Silvery-blue staining sometimes occurs in *Copelandia* species as well as in *Panaeolus cinctulus*.

Green staining in *Copelandia cyanescens* from human handling.

On rare occasions, sometimes *Copelandia* species can produce a green tinge in the caps and stems and a silvery-blue hue when handled or in drying naturally in their habitat.

Copelandia species, when fresh are extremely potent. Chemical studies have shown that some regional and island habitats seem to produce different levels of both psilocine and psilocybine in unusual proportions from one region to another.

While chemical analysis reveals that *Copelandia cyanescens* delivers a most rewarding experience in a one gram-powdered dose, it is said to be equivalent to that of a dried gram of *Psilocybe semilanceata*. Here is a Scanning Electron Microscopy image for those sacred fungi enthusiasts to see just how small the spores of this species are and like *Panaeolus,* they too are lemon-shaped.

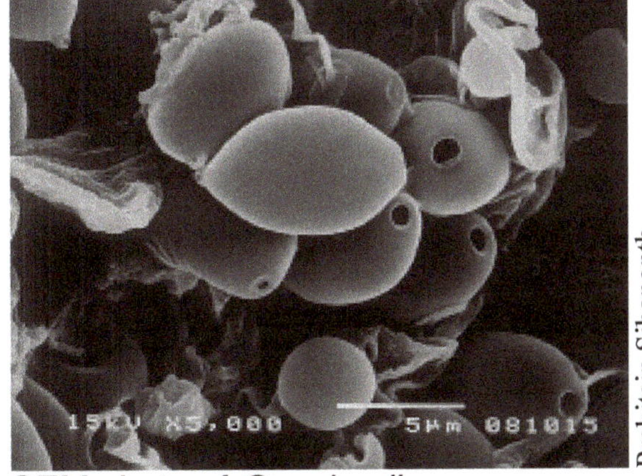

SEM photo of *Copelandia cyanescens.*

Prakitsin Sihanonth

It is possible that certain soil contents of one habitat of study when compared with habitats from other locations may differ. The particular soil content of one habitat may determine the potency and distribution of tryptamine alkaloids to biosynthesize different amounts of active ingredients than those of another habitat with different soil and manured contents.

For instance, chemical analysis of specimens of *Copelandia cyanescens* collected in Queensland, Australia and from several locations in Thailand produced high levels of psilocybine and low levels of psilocine while specimens harvested in Oahu, Hawaii were high in psilocine and low in psilocybine.

Copelandia bispora

Cap: Convex to hemispherical, yellowish-brown to pallid white, becoming cracked or wrinkled and pitted with age.

Gills: Black with white edges.

Stem: Hollow with white fibrils.

Spores: 12-15.5 (15) x 9-10 (11.5) x 6-7μ.

Spore Print: Jet black.

Habitat: Scattered to gregarious in the manure soil where cattle feed or in well-manicured urban lawns, and is rarely observed in pastures or meadows.

Distribution: Occurs sporadically throughout the tropics and neotropics of both hemispheres.

Season: During early spring and fall after heavy rains.

Dosage: 7-10 medium sized specimens to 1-2 grams when dried.

Originally identified from Africa *Copelandia bispors* can be collected on Oahu, Hawaii, Rarely ever growing from the manure of cattle, horses or sheep, it usually fruits in well-fertilized lawns. It loses about 50% potency in drying. In the early 1980s, an unidentified species of *Copelandia* (two specimens only) was observed at a riding stable near Tumwater, Washington.

Copelandia bispora. University of Hawaii's Livestock and Experimental Farm.

Copelandia bispors occurs in Central West Africa, Hawaii, and Florida. Recently it was observed fruiting on a church lawn near Bern, Switzerland. The lawn was completely covered by a rug of *Copelandia bispors*. That rare collection occurred when manured fertilizer purchased from a landscaper in the south of France along the Mediterranean Sea supplied their product to the church in Switzerland. It was observed in several lawns in the San Diego region of Southern California, and is known of in Hawaii, Mexico and some countries in South America.

Copelandia cambodgeniensis

Cap: 1.2-2.5 cm broad, conic-convex at first, soon hemispherical, expanding to broad and eventually plane. Often cracked when dry or in drying. Sometimes the cap which is hygrophanous is seen as golden-brown to chocolate-brown to yellowish-brown with maturity. This species bruises intensely blue when handled or damaged.

Gills: Pallid. Grayish-black to black with age. Mottled. Ascending, uncinate.

Stem: 55-95 mm long by 3.5-5 mm thick. Attached, striate, whitish to crème in color, rapidly bruising blue where injured.

Spores: 8-12 x 7.5-9 x 5.5-6µ.

Spore Print: Blackish brown.

Habitat: Scattered to gregarious on the dung of water buffalo and cattle, in rice paddies, pastures and fields.

Distribution: Widespread throughout the tropics and neotropics in both hemispheres. This species is also known to occur in Florida and Georgia and in both South Asia and Southeast Asia, Indonesia, and in the Caribbean and Pacific/Oceanea Island groups.

Season: Early spring and late fall, especially from October through February.

Dosage: 7 to 10 medium sized mushrooms when fresh and 1-2 grams dried.

Copelandia cambodgeniensis is a strong bluing species with high psilocybine content of .55% and .6% psilocine. Two separate collections were harvested from the manure of cattle near Kualoa Ranch and Coral Kingdom, Kahaluu, Oahu, Hawaii.

Two views of *Copelandia cambodgeniensis*—gold tops and/or blue meanies.

Although there are anywhere from 4-8 species of *Copelandia* in the genera, chemical analysis of *Copelandia cambodgeniensis* revealed it to be an extremely potent species and caution should be taken when consuming this for ludible purposes.

One will come across a good field with lots of *Copelandia* species, usually one to three varieties may be in the same field in different areas or in a paddock next to the one where someone might be searching for them. Some collectors of these mushrooms like to munch down on a few as they come across them while wandering aimlessly harvesting their crops.

What one might see after consuming *Copelandia cambodgeniensis.*

If you happen upon a few and believe like many do, that you can eat a few and then find a lot more, please observe what you might see if you do consume them out in the wild. Remember that it would not be a rewarding experience to be under the influence of these special friends if a law enforcement official came upon you in that condition.

Copelandia cyanescens

Cap: 1.5-3.5 (4) cm broad. Hemispherical to campanulate to convex with maturity. Some times expanding with age, becoming flattened and often cracking. Parched and wrinkled. Yellowish- light brown at first, becoming pallid gray to white in the center. Easily bruising blue when damaged.

Gills: Adnexed, close, thin. Mottled and grayish and black with age.

Stem: (65) 85-115 mm long by 1.5-3 mm thick. Equal to bulbous at base, tubular. Pale and yellowish. Flesh color to light brown towards the apex. Readily turning blue when bruised.

Spores: 12-15 x 8-11 x 6.5-8μ. Smooth, opaque, elliptical. With a germ pore.

Spore Print: Black.

Habitat: Scattered to gregarious in the manure of water buffalo and cattle, gaur, rhino and elephant dung in rice paddies, pastures and fields and sometimes in lawns (but rare in lawns).

Distribution: Widespread throughout the tropics and neotropics in both hemispheres.

Season: Early spring and fall after heavy rains. Flushes run from October through February.

Dosage: 7-10 fresh mushrooms and from 1-2 grams dried.

Copelandia cambodgeniensis and baby buffalo.

Copelandia cyanescens is very potent when fresh, moderately potent when dry, often losing up to more than 50% potency. Hawaiian specimens contained .71% psilocybine, .04% psilocine and 0.1% baeocystine. Comparative analysis in 1993 by Dr. Tjakko Stijve of Nestles showed that *Copelandia cya-*

nescens from Hawaii's and Australia showed that the Hawaiian collections were high in psilocybine while those specimens from Australia showed a higher content of psilocine.

Sometimes spores fall on wild grasses and then cattle consume the alfalfa and other grains in their habitat, which helps spread these fungi into other areas when these animals defecate.

See the image of two blades of wild grass with jet black spore deposit from *Copelandia cyanescens*. This occurred where the cap of the species broke its veil and released the spores directly below it, thus causing the falling spores to land directly on the blades of grass beneath the mushroom.

Cattle eat the grass and on occasion consume the mushrooms. Maybe that is why cows are always laying down in the grass. But more likely they do so because they do not have any chairs to sit on.

Some species of *Copelandia* end up in mulched garden beds when they come to such gardens via powdered manured-fertilizers and even liquid fertilizers. I observed *Copelandia cyanescens* fruiting in mulched garden beds surrounding the Department of Microbiology at Chulalongkorn University in Bangkok. There were so many popping up on a Sunday morning that my friend and colleague, Dr. Prakitsin Sihanonth whose SEM photogra-

Copelandia cyanescens with blue splotches on the cap, a result of elemental damage.

Copelandia cyanescens fruiting in powdered manure used as fertilizer.

phy grace these pages, called me at my condo and informed me to come quickly to the school and bring my camera. When I arrived I was greeted with a most welcomed pleasant surprise. The mushrooms were not only around the Department but we also observed them in gardens that surrounded the Dean's office building on campus.

The cap of the larger specimen of *Copelandia cyanescens* was approximately 2 and ½ inches in diameter. About the same size as the 'Pan Goliath' Suphanburi strain developed by Workman of Spore Works Labs in Tennessee. I can say with good intent that this large cap provided a close friend of mine in Thailand with a very rewarding experience.

Another related species, *Panaeolus cinctulus* has been observed fruiting in mulched garden beds in the Pacific Northwest and Northeastern Coast of the United States. This occurs when liquid fertilizers with the spores of dung-inhabiting species come into contact with the top soils in new gardens. After the gardens are laid out, then wood chips are laid over the topsoil. And sometimes they produce the means to propagate mushrooms where they normally do not occur.

Copelandia tropicalis

Cap: 1.5-2 (2.5) cm broad. Hemispherical to convex to campanulate. Margin incurved in young. Pallid to grayish to yellowish-brown towards the center. Hygrophanous, easily bruising bluish when handled or damaged. Surface smooth to wrinkled in drying.

Gills: Adnexed, uncinate, mottled. Dull grayish black.

Stem: 60-80 (120) mm long by 2-3 mm thick. White to yellowish-brown. Equal to swollen at base with white filaments. Hollow. Readily bruising blue when handled.

Spores: 9-12 x 7,5-9 x 6-7,5μ.

Spore Print: Black.

Habitat: Scattered to gregarious in the manure of water buffalo and cattle in rice paddies, pastures and fields. However, this appears to be a species that grows in and around *Copelandia cyanescens* and without a microscope, macroscopic identification is impossible to differentiate between the two species.

Distribution: Widespread throughout the tropics and neotropics in both hemispheres.

Season: During early spring and fall after heavy rains.

Dosage: 7 to 10 medium sized specimens when fresh and from 1-2 grams dried.

A 20-minute collection of fresh specimens of *Copelandia cyanescens*.

Copelandia tropicalls is often collected along with *Copelandia cyanescens*. When harvesting *Copelandia cyanescens* from a single dung-heap, one may actually have a few specimen of this species. Macroscopically they are similar in appearance and can only be separated with a microscope.

Some ludible users in Florida claim to have fields of this species, however, it is a minor species, rare in most fields in the tropics and neotropics of both hemispheres. This species is rare and only is found when collecting *Copelandia* species that dominate a particular field. In fact most in such fields are probably *Copelandia cyanescens* and maybe out of every 100 specimens or more, there might be a single specimen of *Copelandia tropicalis* in the harvested collections. Only a microscope can separate these species. Once popular, this species was commonly sold in Smart Shoppes in Amsterdam, and throughout the Nederland.

One of three collections of *Copelandia tropicalis* in Hawaii.

FIFTEEN

Panaeolina foenisecii

Panaeolina foenisecii is known as the "hay maker" mushroom and is often confused *Panaeolus cinctulus*. There is confusion about it having psychoactive properties.

In the 1960s, *Panaeolina foenisecii* was analyzed to determine if it is a psilocybian species. Several individual specimens were reported as containing the tryptamine alkaloid psilocybine in small amounts. Many online mushroom aficionados pick *Panaeolina foenisecii* because they believe it to be *Panaeolus cinctulus* which macroscopically resemble one another.

Panaeolina foenisecii, the 'hay mower's mushroom.

The findings by several chemists were wrong in their analytical assessment and their results were false positives, because *Panaeolina foenisecii* was misidentified as *Panaeolus cinctulus*,

In 1996, German mycologist, Ewald Gerhardt re-examined mushrooms belonging to the Genus *Panaeolina, Panaeolus, Anellaria*, and *Copelandia* species; writing the monograph on those families.

Bluing in *Panaeolus cinctulus.*

Those seeking these sacred mushrooms need to understand the confusion between the two species that results in many who pick *Panaeolus foenisecii* believe they have actually found *Panaeolian cinctulus*. The confusion occurs because both species macroscopically resemble one another.

Panaeolina foenisecii is one of the most common, cosmopolitan species of fungi in the world. It can appear scattered or gregarious on lawns, grassy areas, and in meadows. These small LBM mushrooms are frequently observed in the early morning, then wilted or gone by midday. They are often seen in close proximity with other fungus such as *Marasmius oreade*s—the common 'fairy ring' mushroom; *Coprinus* spp., which includes the "inky caps" and "shaggy manes"; and species belonging to the genera's, *Psathyrella* and *Pholiotina*, all which adapted to similar environments—lawns and grasslands.

Panaeolina foenisecii has a striate margin when wet and appears slightly translucent when moist. The cap is also hygrophanous and changes color from a brownish-gray to a medium to dark brown. Sometimes the colors appear to be concentrically streaked, beige almost white to pale at end, in transition with darker, trolled by marginal zone. Said another way, the various bands of color on the caps of *Panaeolina foenisecii* are macroscopically similar to *Panaeolus cinctulus*. Many who have eaten *Panaeolina foenisecii* over the years fervently agreed that it is not active at all.

Two characteristics of *Panaeolina foenisecii* and *Panaeolus cinctulus* that distinguish them from one another so anyone seeking the magic of the mushrooms can correctly identify them. First, the spores and spore deposit of *Panaeolina foenisecii* is

Panaeolina foenisecii are recognized by the many various bands or zones of color on their caps.

chocolate brown, always appearing in grassy areas, meadows and preferably lawns; never fruiting directly from manure. Second, *Panaeolus cinctulus* is known throughout the world as the "weed" fungus and its spore color and deposit is jet black. It can be found in rotted composting haystacks, at riding stables and racetracks and sometimes appears in newly sodded lawns, fruiting only once or twice in a season and then they are gone.

Field guides, mycological and psychological journals and medical reports commonly—and incorrectly— describe *Panaeolus cinctulus* as an active psilocybian mushroom. Even *High Times* magazine devoted several pages featuring *Panaeolina foenisecii* as a common psychoactive fungi found on every lawn in America. Actually, it is not active and not worth collecting

Baby specimens of *Panaeolina foenisecii* reveal their gill structure variations. Children might be prone to pick this species.

There is no recorded medical use of *Panaeolina foenisecii*. Yet, many who have experimented with it claim *Panaeolina foenisecii* promotes relaxation and a tranquil feeling of well-being, which may be triggered by 5hydroxytryptophan, a non-active tryptamine alkaloid neurotransmitter found in various species of mushrooms producing psilocybine and psilocine.

Ethnopharmacologist Jonathan Ott partook of a tea prepared from *Panaeolina foenisecii* then bio-assayed the potion he had prepared and re-

Freshly harvested specimens of *Panaeolina foenisecii* with ruler showing size.

ported no positive psychoactivity present. I and others have reported no activity in *Panaeolina foenisecii*—event when large amounts were used to brew. Some say it is good as a tea to calm one down.

Possibly when *Panaeolina foenisecii* is collected from lawns, taxonomic identification is made, and specimens passed on for chemical identification, other species that macroscopically resemble *Panaeolina foenisecii* are unintentionally included in the collections. According to Dr. Tjakko Stijve of Nestles, "this would explain why some collections of *Panaeolina foenisecii* have been reported to be positive for psilocybin."

SIXTEEN

Panaeolus

The genus *Panaeolus* has a cosmopolitan distribution and several species are known to be psilocybian. Most species of *Panaeolus* are dung inhabiting, although some are terrestrial; occurring in soils, grassy areas and/or composting hay.

Their distinguishing characteristics include a bell-shaped cap, usually conic to convex and not expanding to plain. The stems of these species have no veil or veil-remnants present. They appear to have vertical grooves spiraling down the length of their stems; often covered with whitish fibrils. The stems are of a reddish-brown colored in age. Two active species of *Panaeolus* are known to possess the alkaloids, psilocine and psilocybin in all collections. Baeocystine was detected and extracted from one of these two species, *Panaeolus cinctulus* as renamed by German mycologist, Ewald Gerhardt from *Panaeolus subbalteatus*, the infamous weed fungi.

This species was the cause of several reported unexplained inebriations causing confusion and hallucinations in those who ate them as a food source.

Habitat of *Copelandia* species at Kualoa Ranch on Oahu Island, Hawaii.

Active species have a cosmopolitan distribution and also include *Panaeolus olivaceous.* All chemical studies of *Panaeolus cinctulus* tested positive for active psilocybian alkaloids. The caps of *Panaeolus cinctulus* may be viscid when moist and like the genus *Psilocybe*, they have hollow stems. The primary features used to identify this species are the ornamental bands or zones of colors that form circles around the center of the cap and expanding outwards towards the caps outer edge.

Their spores, like all *Panaeolus* species are black to jet black and their gills are lighter and have white edges. Sometimes one may find two or more species of *Panaeolus* being harvested along with active species of *Copelandia.* This often occurs when a 'shroomer picks several specimens at one site, tossing them into their collection bags. This kind of macroscopic identification is okay if one checks both sides of the cap of the mushroom when picking it. Most first time 'shroomers assume that since the mushrooms they are picking were all growing from the same dung-heap, then they therefore were all the same as the *Copelandia* species they had put in their bags. Those species are shown here but are not fully described.

For example, back in the 1980's I was collecting mushrooms in a pasture at Kualoa Ranch near Chinaman's Hat and Coral Kingdom on Oahu Island in Hawaii. I had just nearly filled a luncheon sandwich bag with a treasure of *Copelandia cyanescens.* I had been going up and down the mountain side with a few friends picking for close to three hours.

It is sad that many 'shroomers toss fresh specimens of *Panaeolus papilionaceus* with their reddish stems and somewhat slightly visible veil remnants into their harvested bags of freshly picked *Copelandia cyanescens.* Neither *Psilocybe coprophila* nor *Panaeolus papilionaceus* are psilocybian fungi. Again, it is really important to stress the need to study the literature of these species to avoid sickness, or possibly even death. When I asked a picker at Kualoa Ranch about why he added those red stemmed *Panaeolus* into his bag he told me if one ate enough of them they would give one a buzz.

The habit of grabbing what is growing from a manure-heap also occurs within the continental United States—mostly in pasture lands from Texas heading eastward to the Florida Coast and as far up north as South Carolina.

Even in the Pacific Northwest I have seen similar stupidity in pastures with people picking liberty caps. One girl had 6-7 different species in her bag of mushrooms. When I saw her collection I told her she would have to dump it. She became very upset to have to pick all over again and asked me to explain to her why?

I had just spent a half hour with her and her sisters showing them what to pick and what not to pick. They were apple pickers from Yakima, Washington and this girl had college behind her. I explained that she may pick something that could make her sick. I further explained that a piece of a toxic species could fall off in the bag and lodge itself inside the cap of an active liberty cap. I explained what could happen if she or a friend were to eat a toxic species.

More irritating, she wasn't paying attention when I pointed out other species in her bag, lifting them out one at a time. I reminded her that I had just spent a lot of time explaining what to pick, what not to pick, how to pick them and how to set them in her bag to protect them. I again stressed that she had at least six different species that were not liberty caps in her bag. She snapped, "Well they all look like mushrooms to me."

Panaeolus antillarum is common throughout the world. It, too, loves the manure of most four-legged ruminants. In the late 1940s, *Panaeolus antillarum* was misidentified after a dozen or more people became inebriated after eating them as food supplements. Of course, in the 1940s, no one in Australia was aware of magic mushrooms.

Three species from the same manure heap. Left to right: (1) *Copelandia cyanescens*; (2) *Panaeolus papilionaceus;* (3) *Psilocybe coprophila*; (4, 5, 6) *Panaeolus papilionaceus.*

Panaeolus antillarum (left), *Psilocybe cubensis* (right).

Local newspapers in Queensland referred to the causative fungi as the "Hysteria fungus". The mushroom that caused discomfort in those who ate them thinking they were "food" was *Copelandia cyanescens.* Sometimes both species can inhabit the same manure at the same time. *Panaeolus antillarum* is not an active species.

On occasion, *Panaeolus antillarum* will appear in a manure-heap along with *Psilocybe cubensis.* When *Panaeolus antillarum* dominate a particular pasture, *Psilocybe cubensis* usually does not appear until *Panaeolus antillarum* has finished their flush in the fields. Then when *Psilocybe cubensis* begins to fruit, it is possible that somewhere in that field, there is a manure-heap with *Panaeolus antillarum* still in it.

It is worrisome that naive people pick and eat mushrooms that they find in the field without knowing what they are eating.

Panaeolus castaneifolius

Cap: The cap of this species is of a chestnut color and is not uniformed in its shape. However, when first changing color in drying, the cap also becomes zonate with bands of colors occurring on the cap as it dries.

Gills: The gills are attached and are adnate to adnexed and are very close, and thin, appearing pallid at first, becoming dark purple to grayish-black when the spores become mature.

Stem: 1-4 cm. This species like *Panaeolus cinctulus* also has vertical grooves spiraling up the length of the stem. The stem, like that of *Psilocybe* species is also hollow.

Spores: 12-15 X 7-9 **μ.**

Spore Print: Black.

Dosage: This species has the same dosage level as that of *Panaeolus cinctulus*. One ounce fresh or from 3-5 grams dried. That could be from 7 larger sized specimens or as many as 12 to twenty fresh specimens all weighing in at one fresh ounce per dosage.

Habitat: Grassy areas in lawns and parks.

Distribution: Very rare in Oregon and Washington yet scattered to gregarious when found. Usually in little groups comprised of small colonies of from 10 to 15 specimens fruiting in individual groups in new lawns.

Season: Summer to fall after rainy periods, preferably in new lawns.

Panaeolus castaneifolius usually has only one or two flushes when it appears in a lawn. For some reason it fruits on two or three occasions in a 3-6 week run, then never returns. I assume it is because of the liquid fertilizers used in the top-soil under the grass or in a sodded lawn. I watched one patch come up three times in six weeks and never returned. Altogether, there may have been at least 12 fresh ounces during that period.

This species is quite a pleasant experience and reportedly quite tranquil yet visual in effects. No nausea has been associated with this species as previously reported in the literature after the consumption of *Panaeolus cinctulus.* Both species at times may resemble one another in color and appearance.

Panaeolus cinctulus

Cap: 2-5.5 cm broad. Fawn-colored to reddish-brown, zonate from the outer edge of the cap with several bands of reddish-brown colors towards the center. Sometimes with a slight umbo. Hygrophanous, fading to a straw yellow to pallid in drying to a pallid dull white. Margin slightly incurved when young, often becoming pitted and wrinkled with age. And with age, the cap becomes flat turning slightly upwards in some collections.

Gills: Adnate and slightly ventricose. Brownish to black with white edges.

Stem: 4-10 cm x 2-7 mm. Reddish brown with vertical grooves running down the length of the stem. Hollow with short white fibrils. Sometimes bluing at base of the stem.

Spores: 11.5-14 x 7.5-9.5 μ

Spore Print: Jet black.

Dosage: 2-5 large specimens or 20-30 small specimens weighing at least one fresh ounce. 3-5 grams dried. This species has about the same average potency as *Psilocybe cubensis*.

Season: February through May during the spring rains and from mid-August through September.

Habitat: On dung, rotted and/or composting hay. Also in lawns, pasture lands, riding stables and race tracks, in horse manure and horse manure mixed with stable shavings. Fruits in the early spring and late fall. This species occurs in most of the United States and Canada and has a worldwide distribution on 5 continents.

Distribution: Cosmopolitan throughout 5 continents. It is common in Western Oregon, Washington and British Columbia, Canada; as well as in Mexico. This species also occurs along the entire East Coast of America, and much of Europe and Asia. While this species have been observe in small amounts from manure heaps on Oahu, Maui, and the Big Island of Hawaii, it is rather rarer in Hawaii than elsewhere.

The Weed Mushroom

Panaeolus subbalteatus, renamed, *Panaeolus cinctulus*, was originally known to growers of commercial edible mushrooms as the "weed" mushroom. This species occurs abundantly in haystacks in the Eugene-Corvallis region of Oregon and to a somewhat lesser degree in manure and lawns. In the Nederland, Fresh Mushrooms of Tiel, one of the original legal magic mushroom farms in the Nederland, produced more than 20,000 kilos per month and were marketed and sold to tourists and locals in most Smart Shoppes in the Nederland.

Panaeolus cinctulus is an entheogenic species that contains the psychomimetic indole alkaloids psilocybin, psilocin and baeocystin. Noted mycologists Rolf Singer and Alexander H. Smith likened this species as but "one of a number of weed fungi [like crab grass is to grass] found spontaneously like weeds in beds of the cultivated commercial white mushroom, *Agaricus bisporis* — your common grocery store mushroom."

During the past 120-years, *Panaeolus cinctulus* has been referred to by members of the mycological community and mushroom growers of edible species by many different binomials, including *Panaeolus venonosus*—poisonous mushroom. Synonyms include *Panaeolus rufus, Panaeolus semigloblatus*, and *Panaeolus variabilis*. It was once considered to be conspecific with *Panaeolus papilionaceus.*

The latter species is commonly referred to as the "butterfly" mushroom; however, *Panaeolus papilionaceus* is not an active species although many field guides say that it is.

Panaeolus cinctulus on a lawn, Seattle, Washington.

Since the early 1900's, numerous intoxications occurred when *Panaeolus cinctulus* was accidentally consumed as an edible variety. Early reports regarding accidental inebriations from *Panaeolus* species date back to the Chin dynasty—2nd century A.D.—and the 11th century in Japan. Many ancient Chinese herbal medicine books described unknown species of *Panaeolus* as the cause of a laughing sickness and describe cures under the heading of "Cures for the laughing sickness." A remedy for this laughing malady requires a potion consisting of an infusion of water, which has been filtered through topsoil. The inflicted party drinks the potion to alleviate the intense laughter after accidentally or purposely ingesting psilocybian fungi.

Panaeolus cinctulus is a cosmopolitan species found all over the world. It is common in the dung of cattle and composting hay and/or haystacks. Other habitats include lawns, open fields and riding stables. In the Pacific Northwest of the United States, its season extends from late February through early June and again in August and September. *Panaeolus cinctulus* fruits abundantly in rotted haystacks in the Willamette Valley in Oregon. In the Hawaiian archipelago, *Panaeolus cinctulus* is abundant in cow manure at the 3000-foot elevation above and below Kula highway on Maui Island. This species also has a worldwide distribution depending on the weather conditions.

Identifying *Panaeolus cinctulus*

In 1982, I was on a mushroom foray in a pasture, in Kent, Washington, a field where I had previously studied the growth, development and various habitats of the "liberty cap" mushroom—*Psilocybe semilanceata*. The 'liberty cap' mushroom is known to be the most commonly sought after mushroom in the Pacific Northwest. The 'liberty cap is common from Quebec to Southern Ontario and eastward along the Coast of both Canada and upper state New York, and northward towards Nova Scotia and beyond. During that foray I came upon a most startling discovery, one that I never expected would ever happen to me.

There, right in front of my eyes, was a tiny grouping of what appeared to me to be some very small mushrooms which

Panaeolus papilionaceus in horse manure and composting hay mixed with stable shavings.

I believed might possibly contain the hallucinogenic alkaloids, psilocybine and psilocine.

Over the years, my day-by-day field research was finally paying off. It had become somewhat of a daily habit that I ritualistically enjoyed. I had gained a very deep insight in identifying many varieties of fungi and my knowledge of species had tremendously grown since I first discovered the "liberty cap" mushroom back in the early 1970s.

It was in the early part of April and I had been wandering from field to field for about three hours. On this particularly cloudy and sometimes rainy spring day, I came upon and espied a fairly small sized grouping of multi-banded fungi—marked by zones of color on their caps. I was enchanted by their fresh appearance. They were in a cluster and appeared to be huddling together like a family trying to keep themselves warm. The mushrooms seemed to be asking the sky to bring them more fresh rain so they could grow tall, as if they were trying to reach out to the heavens above them.

One of the first notable features I observed about the mushrooms while gazing at their radiance was that they were growing directly out of a dung heap or "cow pie".

Gazing at this wonderful symbiosis of mushroom and dung, I realized the mushrooms might possess a celestial energy. It was as if they were telepathic, speaking to me in a language only they and I knew. I could feel their aura and I knew they were been calling me to visit them. They were inviting me to their home so that I could experience all that they were; even inviting me to pick them from their habitat they knew so well. I felt that they transcended to me warmth that only I knew and the wind seemed to whisper over and over, “Pick me, pick me. Yes pick me if you dare.”

Within a few seconds, beginning from that very moment when my eyes first gazed upon their presence in the dung, a slight grin appeared across my face and I smiled as my heart fluttered and palpitated exceedingly faster than it normally did. I was flushed with excitement because I realized the potential these little mushrooms held for one such as I who had humbly wandered into their time and space of existence on this green little planet which we call Earth.

I knelt down on the ground next to the mushrooms. As I did, my knees melted into the soft wet moist dewy grass around their humble home of a cow pie. I took several photographs of the fungi as I scanned the caps, gills, and stems of the mushrooms, keying the fungi into their genera and species.

First, I noticed the pileus or caps of the mushrooms were somewhat zonate, that is, they had layered zones of different shades of color running from the outer edges of the cap towards the center. Each cap was similar in appearance, each exhibiting several shades of a reddish-brown to a pallid tan tone. Later, an hour after the rain had stopped; I dried the mushrooms in the sun. Then I noticed a color change had occurred. It transformed their radiance from a cinnamon reddish-brown—sometimes a fawn color—to a light copper brown in the center of the cap and then they dries to a pallid white tone.

The center of the caps on two of the mushrooms looked knobby. Eventually the color of the caps faded completely to a pallid off whitish-gray tone. In some specimens the caps became pitted, wrinkled and parched as they dried. The younger spec-

Angry ‘Shroom

Panaeolus cinctulus fruiting from rotted composting hay with manure and stable shavings.

imens I observed were bell shaped or ovate—some were even convexed to umbonate in age. The margins on some of the caps were slightly incurved but did not seem to be translucent—viscid when moist—like their cousins the Psilocybes.

I turned over the pileus—cap—I was holding and took out my portable scissors from inside of my back pack. I cut the stem from the cap and placed it, with gill plates facing down, onto white paper I had extracted from my back pack to make a spore print to properly identify the genus to which the mushrooms belonged. Then I placed a small jar over the mushroom cap so the spores would fall properly down onto the paper and not blow away.

This procedure is an important step for the amateur mycologist who wishes to avoid an unpleasant accidental intoxication of a possible poisonous species of mushroom. It is also an important step in keying to genus, various species of fungi. Proper field identification of a fungi species is necessary.

After twenty minutes I lifted the small jar from off the paper and removed the mushroom cap to revealed the exact color the spore print had produced. I was astonished to find that my mushroom cap had created a beautiful perfectly-shaped spore print—resembling a spiraling eye which was totally jet black.

Black spores are representative of several different genera *Coprinus*—inky caps—and *Panaeolus*, which include the cosmopolitan genus *Copelandia* and *Anellaria*.

Panaeolus cinctulus in manured soil near salt shed. Kent, Washington.

I checked the gills of the cap I had used to produce the spore print and examined the gills and their structure. I noticed the edges of the gills were white and somewhat variegated or mottled. The margin of the cap seemed to overlap the gills.

I examined the end of the stem I had earlier cut from the

Mushroom hunter named Shannon at Kualoa Ranch, Oahu, Hawaii.

mushroom cap to determine if it was hollow. It was. This is another common feature in both *Panaeolus* and *Psilocybe* species. The color of the stem ranged from a dark reddish-brown to a light fawn color and appeared to have vertical lines running like spirals up and down the stem, which was covered with white fibrils. No veil or remnants of a veil were present. The base of the stem was covered with a fine fluffy patch of white mycelium with threads of mycelia protruding around its bulbous bottom.

Suddenly my eyes sparkled, lighting up like a bright comet streaking across the Washington skyline. Even though it was now sunny and dry, I saw a rainbow in the distance from the previous rain south of Tukwila, Washington in beautiful valley of pasture lands.

I noticed a tiny tinge of heavenly azure blue running along the base of the bulbous stem from where I had plucked it from out of the dung. Only then did I realize that this small black agaric fungi I had stumbled upon during my humble wanderings was none other than the infamous "weed" fungus *Panaeolus cinctulus*; an active psilocybian species.

That is how I found my first *Panaeolus* mushroom. Of course, there were not enough of the mushrooms to get high, but I was not in a hurry to take a small dosage.

Looking back, I remembered that day in Hawaii at Kualoa Ranch when my friends were overwhelmed with excitement as each was able to fill a sandwich bag of *Copelandia cyanescens*. Not one person had put any specimens of *Panaeolus papilionaceus* into their bags. Good people pick good mushrooms. When we left the ranch we headed up to the North Shore to a big outdoor party with friends I had taken picking. They learned how to harvest to keep bad inactive mushrooms from entering their bag of good healthy mushrooms.

SEVENTEEN

Little Brown Mushrooms

My earliest memory of mushrooms entering my conscious mind occurred on my tenth birthday. On that day, I was looking forward to gorging myself on my favorite food, Chop Suey with dried noodles over rice. I liked it so much that my mother treated my sister and me with a birthday dinner in Chicago's Chinatown district.

After my mom ordered our food, the waitress went back to the kitchen and soon returned with three bowls of soup. I remember that the soup was quite delicious. When the waitress returned with three cups of tea, I told her how much I enjoyed the soup and asked what kind it was and she said it was "mushroom soup."

Suddenly, I threw up on the table and all over the waitress's apron. Some of the gurgitation even splattered onto my sister. Just the word "mushroom" frightened me into vomiting.

As I think back to that incident so long ago, I wonder why—at such an early age—I was so mycophobic about that soup and its contents.I suspect that the mushrooms that triggered vomiting were probably dehydrated *Shitake* mushrooms.

Soup with *Shitake* mushrooms

My first introduction into the magical world of fungi was what not to eat! Who would have guessed that twenty some years later I would love the very mushrooms I was afraid to eat again?

Many small mushrooms that grow in lawns are so numerous, many mycologists think they are not worth photographing or collecting. Some mycologists admit that many species of small mushrooms are very hard to identify. Since they are small, mushroom hunters throughout the world call them "little brown mushrooms"—or LBM's.

LBM is a current popular cultural acronym used as slang by mycologists (both professional and amateurs) when referring to any little brown mushroom that grows in grassy areas or in mulched garden beds layered with wood chips.

Little brown mushrooms or LBM's is not an academic description. Rather it refers to many species of mushrooms that are small and are not considered by mushroom hunters as meaty enough to be prepared and served at an evening meal.

Even though called little "brown" mushrooms, not all LBM's are brown. Many small species belong to different families and their caps and gills may be brown to cinnamon colored, or white; and some caps in aging or drying will fade from their original color to that of an off-white shade or even a straw-yellow color. However, several small sized species of magic mushrooms also occur in lawns and wood chips and are also referred to as LBM's.

Non-active LBM varieties of *Pholiotina* species.

Non-active LBM wood-chip varieties of *Pholiotina* species.

Online community mushroom forums often have members offering identifications to new members asking for mushroom ID's of species they find while on a walk-about. On many occasions, some members, although wanting to be helpful, misidentify the species in question. For those individuals who hunt the magic species that occur in the same lawns or mulched garden beds where several different species of LBM's are found, one should realize that while some of those small species can macroscopically be identified by an experienced mushroom hunter, only a microscope can separate the various LBM species found in lawns and mulched garden beds.

Some species found in lawns and in wood chip habitats may be toxic but not quite deadly so may cause nausea, diarrhea, gastric discomfort, and vomiting But one particular species that sometimes occurs in lawns and wood chips that is toxic and deadly is *Pholiotina filaris*. This orangey to cinnamon colored cap and rusty orangey gills and spore deposit has deadly toxins known to occur in *Amanita phalloides* and in at least three spe-

Pholiotina cyanopoda in a damp swampy sphagnum-mossy habitat.

cies of *Galerina.* Such toxins are common in the small conical to flat-capped lawn and wood chip species, *Pholiotina filaris*, also discussed in the chapter on poisonous look-a-like species.

Because there are two active psilocybian species of *Pholiotina* that grow in lawns, I again caution anyone searching for those active species of *Pholiotina*, to avoid collecting them unless you have a good understanding of the species you come across when out on a foray. Never forget that many species look-a-like and often may be growing next to one another.

Always remember that there are more active *Psilocybe* species in North America and Mexico that can be found in urban and suburban settings than in any other region of the world. These species can grow in many different environmental settings and are easy and safe to recognize if happened upon by those interested in experienced their magic. And while some species of *Psilocybe* are referred to as LBM mushrooms, they are still treasured by those who find and harvest them.

In North America, two species of *Pholiotina* contain the alkaloids psilocine and psilocybine. And while these particular mushrooms have orangey to cinnamon colored gills, they are considered by most mycologists as LBM's.

Pholiotina cyanopoda

Cap: .7-1.2 (2-5) cm broad. The cap of *Pholiotina cyanopoda* is somewhat hemispherical to convex, expanding to a broad convexed-shape with age; eventually becoming conic. The margin appears to be translucent and striate when moist. The color of the cap ranges from a yellow-umber to a cinnamon or reddish-cinnamon color to a dark orangey-cinnamon color with age. At times, the cap will fade to an off-white color.

Gills: The gills of *Pholiotina cyanopoda* are adnexed, close and broad. They are of a dull rusty brown color that has a white fringe circling along the outer margin of the cap.

Stem: The stem of *Pholiotina cyanopoda* is short at about 20-40 mm long x 1-1.4 thick. This is a small species and usually never grows to a height of more than three inches.

Spores: The spores of *Pholiotina cyanopoda* range in size from 6.5-7.5 (.5) x 4.5-5 **µ.**

Spore Print: Rusty brown.

Habitat: This species appears scattered in grassy areas and fields, often growing from sphagnum moss along streams and riverbank where sheep and cattle graze, and sometimes in newly sodded lawns.

Distribution: Oregon, Washington, British Columbia, Canada; Michigan and the Northeastern United States and into parts of Southern Ontario, Canada; and then east to the Atlantic Ocean.

Season: Summer and fall.

Dosage: The proper dosage for *Pholiotina cyanopoda* is from 40 to 50 small specimens weighing about ⅓ of a fresh ounce. That would be approximately 2 to 3 doses per fresh ounce.

Pholiotina cyanopoda was formerly known as *Conocybe cyanopus* (Latin for cone head–blue face). This is a very small mushroom that never grows taller than 3 inches in height. This species can be found in the Pacific Northwest of the United States in the spring to summer and then the early fall months. They can be found in new sodded lawns in parks and in lawns around new condos and restaurants and even on the lawns of newly constructed government buildings. They are known to occur in abundance in fields where sheep graze along streams and riverbanks fruiting out of a sphagnum moss and grassy habitat.

Usually the mushrooms are below the height of the grass so that one has to sometimes look directly straight down into the grass in order to be able to see them. I found my first patch of *Pholiotina cyanopoda* off of Interstate I-5 at the North Santiam exit to Salem, Oregon in the spring of 1978. They were fruiting from moss in a field of sheep grazing along a stream near the freeway exit.

During the past 36-years I have only came across this species four times. The cap of this species is cinnamon colored to a bright shade of orange that becomes a darker orange in age and it has a watery to off-white colored stem with an enlarged bulbous base that is already blue when lifted from the ground.

Caleb Brown

Bluing at the base of the stem in *Pholiotina cyanopoda.*

Sometimes the stems of *Pholiotina cyanopoda* may appear to be clear like water but are somewhere in between clear to clear and pale white. Because of the species macroscopic resemblance to some of the deadly species of fungi such as *Pholiotina filaris* (see chapter on poisonous look-a-like species), it is my opinion that 'shroom voyagers in search of magic species should be well advised to avoid picking this LBM unless one is a qualified mycologist. If so then one could readily identify it and separate it from the deadly species that one might come across in their travels while seeking out these fungi.

Pholiotina cyanopoda may also macroscopically resemble other deadly related species that might exist in the genus *Pholiotina* or possibly even some of the deadly *Galerina* species as well. Sometimes deadly look-a-like species are found in lawns growing alongside of fresh specimens of both *Psilocybe stuntzii* and *Psilocybe baeocystis.* And they might even grow directly under the caps of those magic fungi when harvesting small handfuls of such active species. That can occur when fresh mushrooms are not fully examined on both sides when harvested and then just dropped into a collection container. Always turn the mushroom upside down to check the color of the gills and make sure that all the specimens you collect are the real thing..

Pholiotina filaris has also been observe fruiting in wood chipped mulched garden beds where *Psilocybe cyanescens, Psilocybe baeocystis, Psilocybe stuntzii, Psilocybe ovoideocystidiata, Psilocybe allenii,* and other potent cold weather species fruit during the fall to winter months. One notable feature of *Pholiotina filaris* is that it has a white veil remnant on the stem of the species; an annulus that stays on the stem after the cap has broken open. Also, the conical shape of the cap will eventually become flat in age with an umbo or protrude in the center of the cap.

Ron Pastorino

Pholiotina filaris

A profound religious experience occurred in Eugene, Oregon in 1976 with this species when a couple each consumed close to 75 fresh mushrooms weighing between ⅓ to ½ of a fresh ounce. Several months later I ran into my friends who I knew had consumed a handful each of the mushrooms. It had been their first mushroom voyage and one day I came across them on a sunny afternoon where they were having a yard sale on their front lawn. On one of their tables I noticed five bongs and a two beautiful hand-carved Ivory

Caleb Brown

Pholiotina smithii

meerschaum pipes for sale. My friend said they had bought those pipes years before while vacationing in Stockholm.

When I asked them why they were selling their bongs and pipes, they informed me of their experience while under the influence of the mushrooms they had eaten months before and admitted that after their voyage, they had both became stout devout Christians and had no ill will about their experience. In fact they informed me that eating those mushrooms had changed their lives for the better; admitting that the day after their rather somewhat unique and very intense visual experience, they sought out a friend's family minister whom they had not seen in years and they asked him to convert them back to their Christian roots. They also said that the mushrooms were not a sinful experience and that they should never be illegal because they brought them back to their Lord.

Pholiotina smithii

Like *Pholiotina cyanopoda, Pholiotina smithii* grows during the early spring to summer often fruiting in grassy wet damp areas where sphagnum moss is common. That includes such habitats as fields and pasture lands situated along streams and riverbanks;

sometimes occurring in mossy areas with top-soil covered in wood chips layered in mulched garden beds.

While this species lacks a veil or remnants of a veil, its deadly cousin, *Pholiotina filaris* does have a pronounced veil remnant. However, *Pholiotina filaris* may lose its veil remnants with age or from elemental damage and thus both magic and deadly toxic species may both resemble one another. I have only found this species twice in the Pacific Northwest during the past 36-years.

Cap: The caps of *Pholiotina smithii* are .3-1 (1-3) cm broad. They are very hemispherical to convex, easily expanding to broadly convex with age, sometimes conic. The margin is translucent and striate when moist. The color of *Pholiotina smithii*'s caps range from a yellowish-umber shade to a cinnamon reddish-cinnamon shade in age.

Gills: The gills of *Pholiotina smithii* are adnate to adnexed with dull rusty brown tones and a white fringe circling along the margin's edge.

Stem: The stem ranges in length and width from 10-50 (70) mm long by .75-1 (1.5) mm thick. The color is an odd-white shade that becomes a light pallid yellowish-brown and somewhat grayish at its base. It is covered with fine to smooth fibrils. The base of the stem, is the same as found in *Pholiotina cyanopoda.* It also has a tinge of azure-blue after being harvested by human handling.

Spores: The spores of *Pholiotina cyanopoda* range in size from (6.5) 7-9 by 4-4.5 (5) µ.

Spore Print: Rusty brown.

Habitat: Scattered in grassy areas, lawns and fields in mossy areas of sphagnum moss in damp wet places.

Distribution: Oregon, Washington, and British Columbia, Canada. It was also collected in Michigan State by the late Dr. Alexander Smith. It is possible that this species occurs in several northern states from Minnesota to Maine and South into northern New York and Pennsylvania. So far this species has not been reported from Europe.

Season: Summer and fall.

As noted, these two species are also classified as an LBM's and *Pholiotina cyanopoda* and *Pholiotina smithii* are both macroscopically similar in appearance and can only be distinguished from one another by microscopic study or by a trained mycologist who knows the genus.

Because of its macroscopic resemblance to the deadly species *Pholiotina filaris,* I again urge perspective voyagers to avoid this species.

To be on the safe side try to remember that there are a lot of *Psilocybe* species in the United States, Canada and Mexico that have chocolate brown to purple-brown spore deposits and *Copelandia* and *Panaeolus* species that have jet black spore deposits and they are easy to identify and present no danger to those who search for them rather than these *Pholiotina* species described here in this chapter.

Dosage: 40 to 50 small specimens. *Pholiotina smithii* also has the same potency level as that of *Pholiotina cyanopoda.* These are very small mushrooms and a normal dosage can weigh in at 1/3 of a fresh ounce. They do not grow taller than 3-inches in height. So they do not weigh very much at all. There seems to be approximately 3-4 doses per fresh ounce.

Albert Hoffman and Gordon Wasson.

EIGHTEEN

Big Laughing Gyms

Gymnopilus is a family of mushrooms with at least 8 known entheogenic species, and while these mushrooms are psilocybian, they are not recommended for ludible use because sometimes macroscopic characteristics that may mimic, in the young stages, some of the deadly *Galerina* mushrooms. They are also a poor substitute for the active *Psilocybe* species of which several grow quite abundantly throughout the United States, Canada and Mexico.

Gymnopilus species are found fruiting gregariously on rotten wood, often in dense clusters on fallen tree stumps and in woodchips, appearing during and after the early fall rains and everywhere that decaying wood can be found.

One species that many 'shroomers are aware of is *Gymnopilus junonius*, formerly known as *Gymnopilus spectabilis*. This is a species that macroscopically resembles the well-prized edible species *Armillaria mellea,* known by edible mushroom hunters as the "honey mushroom."

During the past 5 years, certain species of *Gymnopilus* have been purposely sought out by ludible users who come seeking magic mushrooms, especially in States where *Psilocybe* species are not known

Joshua Hutchins

Gymnopilus junonius.

to occur or are very rare and hard to find. This species is often referred to on many Internet mushroom forums where ludible users of these magic species refer to *Gymnopilus* as "big laughing gyms." That acronym was first used by Japanese mushroom hunters to describe the effects of incessant laughter often described in the medical literature as one of the more pleasurable symptoms attributed to a *psilocybian* inebriation.

In the early 1980s, I was fortunate to participate as a novice at the first four Myco-Media mushroom conferences held at Orcas Island in the San Juan's of the Pacific Northwest United States. At one of those early Myco-Media conferences I had the fortune to sample a small portion of this mushroom and thought that this will really be easy for me.

I vividly recalled that of all the mushroom voyages I had entered into, not once was I deterred by someone telling me that the mushrooms tasted like shit or that they were just too nasty tasting to eat. "OMG, I thought out loud to myself. No wonder the Aztec's served and consumed chocolate and honey with these special mushrooms during Moctozuma's coronation."

However, while I did not experience any of the effects of the alkaloids in that pea sized bite, I thought about what would happen if the mushrooms had been a potent species so I knew that no matter how bad the taste, that the end results of what was about to happen would be well worth the wait as I had no trouble downing a piece of this species.

Well! I had to admit that Dr. Pollock—as he informed me—was absolutely right about the noxious taste of *Gymnopilus junonius*. It really was, as he had stated, extremely acrid and very bitter. However, over the past 38-years I had found and identified four active species of *Gymnopilus,* not once did I ever have a desire to eat any of those huge fungi that were historically referred to in Japanese, Chinese and English as those 'big laughing gyms.'

Jason Granquist.

Armillaria mellea
(the honey mushroom)

During the past hundred and fifty years, several unidentified fungal species had been reported in journals and diaries of explorers, botanists, seaman, physicians, many of whom reported over the centuries, tales of mushroom inebriations that caused very colorful visual hallucinations, possible temporary madness, incessant laughter, frenzied and wild dancing; and even displays of very intense sexual activity. It was because of these reports that I sought to learn all that was known about them and so I became a seeker and follower of these special mushrooms and their magic and I did learn about them and then I shared that knowledge with others.

The historical significance of these mushrooms is now a part of our culture. The facts confirm that even the genus *Gymnopilus* has a recorded history of accidental inebriations that date to the Chin Dynasty during the 2nd century A.D. in China. One early Chinese Herbal Remedy tomb described a strange illness in which the treatment was referred to as 'cures for the laughing sickness.'

Obviously this symptom was in reference to the "incessant laughter" that is one of many of the common effects attributed to a *psilocybian* experience. These outbreaks of laughter were known to the Chinese as the "laughing sickness." To cure this illness, one must prepare an infusion of earth with water and then drink the liquid after it has been strained through some clothe. The end result would then stop the afflicted victims mushroom inebriations of the intense incessant laughter brought on when eating these mushrooms.

In Japan during the 11th century A.D., there is a folk tale that describes an inebriation that may or may not have been caused by a meal of *Gymnopilus junonius*. In Japan, they have a common epithet for what is believed to be *Gymnopilus junonius,* or a similar active related species. In one book of ancient folktales

Linda Deer.
Dr. Steven H. Pollock

The Lady of the 'Shroom.

Gymnopilus junonius was referred to by the epithet, *waraitake* or "laughing mushroom." That species was first believed to have been *Panaeolus papilionaceus,* a species now known as a non-active mushroom. On the other hand, the epithet, ōwaraitake was used to describe a larger mushroom found near Maple trees and referred to it as a 'big laughing mushroom.' In the United States, Canada, Australia/NZ and much of Europe, *Gymnopilus junonius* is referred to by members of the online mushroom community as 'laughing gyms.'

The suggested psilocybian properties of *Gymnopilus junonius* were first brought to the attention of the public through the published papers of ethnomycologist R. Gordon Wasson and author Jeremy Sanford. Both investigators had found in the Japanese literature, a book of folk lore that told of inebriations caused by certain mushrooms. One tale told of a group of Buddhist nuns who became lost in the mountains of Kyoto stands out as a classic tale of psilocybian mushroom inebriation; a story of a small group of nuns who found themselves alone in the dark on a mountain trail who became lost and feared that they would starved to death and parish overnight in the foothills of Kyoto.

In the darkness of the forest floor, the trees stood alone, and the nuns soon became hungry; fearing that they might die due to a lack of food. When I first read of this incident, I wondered why the nuns, who had missed there afternoon and evening meals, believed that they could starve and die from not eating their daily bread.

Before too long, the nuns came upon some mushrooms that grew near the tress and knowing full well that the species they found had caused those who ate them to laugh, sing, and dance so well; so the nuns roasted the mushrooms and immediately ate some of the mushrooms what they had found, collected and roasted. After a while, once the effects of the mushrooms began to commence, the nuns, still very cold, saw a light up the mountainside and heading up the mountain where they eventually came across a small band of wood-cutters who had also become lost in the woods.

As they met, the woodcutters were surprise at the strange behavior exhibited by the nuns who were laughing and dancing wildly around the campfire. The wood cutters, also very hungry asked the nuns why they were acting the way they did and the nuns told the wood cutters of the mushrooms that they had roasted and eaten. So the nuns shared with the woodsmen, a meal of the roasted wild mushrooms that they had earlier gathered in the mountains.

Once the woodcutters had consumed the mushrooms, they then joined the nuns who were still acting very peculiar and then both the nuns and the woodcutters proceeded to happily dance around the campfire all night long while in a frenzied state of ecstatic inebriation.

Come morning, the nuns and the wood-cutters, both extremely exhausted from their all night sequelae of a magic mushroom banquet and dance soon returned to their perspective villages; somewhat shaken, but happy to be in good spirits from their all night dancing celebration.

Joshua Hutchins.

Gymnopilus junonius. Observe the blue-green stain from the stem being damaged.

Ron Pastorino.

The gill side of *Gymnopilus junonius* has a scorpion scoping out a possible inebriation or just waiting for a meal to pass by

At the time of this tale during the 11th Century, the mushrooms in question were referred to as *maitake*, an epithet implying that they were known as the 'dancing mushrooms.' Today, in Japan, the edible species referred to as *maitake* was examined and no active tryptamine derivatives have been detected in the species known as *maitake*—dancing mushrooms—and the suspected species was more than likely, *Gymnopilus junonius*, or a related species of *Gymnopilus*.

Throughout the last two millennia, *Gymnopilus junonius* was reported as the probable cause of numerous accidental inebriations that probably first occurred when early humankind foraged for edible vegetative foods as well as the fungal species they came across while hunting for food to feed their nomadic tribal groups.

Over the years I have observed *Gymnopilus junonius* and other related species being consumed by young adults who have all reported this species as being one of the most bitterly tasting wild mushrooms that one might ever put into their mouths. Ludible users have often complained about the putrid and acrid taste of this species, arguing that even a small bite-sized amount will cause one's lips to pucker up for a period of 10 minutes or longer after nibbling on a pea sized piece of this species.

Gymnopilus aeruginosus

In the United States during the late 1930s and 1940s, this species resulted in some inebriation's that were chronicled in the academic literature; One woman who had experience intense hallucinations after consuming a meal of *Gymnopilus junonius* had conveyed to her doctor that "if this is the way one were to die from mushroom poisoning, then she was all for it."

Besides the presence of psilocybine in *Gymnopilus junonius,* other entheogenic compounds were discovered to be present in *Gymnopilus junonius*. One such compound was bis-noryangonin, an active substance that is structurally related to the alpha-pyrones and hispidine found in Kava—*Piper methysticum*—a Polynesian Pacific Island somatic-inebriating compound.

In addition to *Gymnopilus junonius*, several other specie of this genera have also been chemically investigated and there appears to be at least 4 or more other specie of this genus that are psilocybian, including some recent discoveries of related species from Brazil.

INOCYBE SPECIES

The genus *Inocybe* has at least 5-6 species that possess the alkaloids psilocine and psilocybine. However, in the1990s, Dr. Jochen Gartz of the University in Leipzig, Germany, discovered a new tryptamine alkaloid found in *Inocybe aeruginascens* that he named aeruginascin[e]. However, the majority of *Inocybe* species are very toxic—containing muscarine and other possible toxins.

Gymnopilus aeruginosus

Alan Rockefeller

Gymnopilus subpurpuratus

It is important to note that many species of *Inocybe* possess muscarine, a toxin that causes stomach distress, vomiting, and diarrhea, yet those *Inocybe* species that contain the active tryptamine alkaloids psilocine and psilocybine do not possess muscarine. Nor are any such toxins found in *Galerina steglichii* that also possesses psilocine and psilocybine. Yet there are also deadly amatoxins and phalatoxins in several species of *Galerina* that are deadly, so again, I asked those who love these mushrooms. But because of the toxicity found within this family of mushrooms, I again recommend that all should please stay away from the *Inocybe* and *Galerina* species.

PLUTEUS SPECIES

Another family with three to six known active species is *Pluteus* (pink-gilled fungi and spore deposit). In the United States, *Pluteus salicinus* is known from Central to Southern Illinois. It was later analyzed and found to contain several psilocybian alkaloids. Similar finds of active *Pluteus* show species from Europe, as well as three new species that were recently found in the Brazilian State of Paraná. Again, I stress the necessity of learning what not to pick and only adhering to the active species described by me in this book.

To those interested in what not to pick, then all should take caution to the wind and remind one another that there are more than 25 active psilocybian species in North America and more than 40 in Mesoamerica. Such species can be easily identified by their chocolate-brown to dark purplish-brown spore deposit color.

Caleb Brown

Gymnopilus viridans

And do not forget that there are at least 4-8 known species of *Copelandia* and at least 3 active species of *Panaeolus*, all of which produce a jet-black spore deposit and these black-spored mushrooms occur primarily in the manure of most four-legged ruminants and of course are very easy to identify due to their intense bluing reaction when handled or damaged from natural elements..

Tjakko Stijve.

Inocybe haemacta.

To insure the safety of those who love these psilocybian fungi, whether they be used to search for one's own religious awakenings or for ludible use, then please make sure that all perspective 'shroomers be advised to avoid all mushrooms with orangey-rusty-brown spore deposits or print colors, as well as all mushroom species with white gills and a white spore deposit. Be sure to only harvest the easy to find species described herein that are found in the genera's, *Psilocybe, Copelandia*, and *Panaeolus*.

NINETEEN

Psilocybe

The genus *Psilocybe* is large, consisting of more than 180 known species, many which are entheogenic. These species have a wide variety of habitats, including dung, manured soil, sandy soil, pastures, meadows, lawns, woods, among decayed twigs and leaves, and in both urban and suburban landscaped areas that include wood chips—preferably alder and other mixed hardwoods.

Psilocybe species share common macroscopic characteristics that occur within the genera, which include a conic to bell-shaped to convex cap, often with a nipple, umbo or protrude at the very center of the top of the cap. While the shapes of the cap vary, not all caps will have a nipple, umbo or protrude.

Margins of the caps are often incurved when young. Some caps become convex and flat with age, while others may become wavy. Many of the caps in the genus *Psilocybe* appear viscid when moist and their margins tend to be translucent-striate when moist—meaning that the lines of the gill plates are visible on the caps when they are moist. *Psilocybe* species have a viscid pellicle, which is a film or skin-like membrane, that when moist may be lifted and easily separated from the cap.

The colors of the caps vary and range from a dark olive brown or chestnut rusty color when fresh to a pallid straw-yellow when dried. The caps are hygrophanous, meaning that they change color as they dry. A slight blue staining may occur along the outer edges of the caps when damaged. In some species this bluing is very intense. The color of the gills range from a light cinnamon brown to dark chocolate or dark purple brown in age.

Psilocybe stuntzii with striate margins along the outer edges of the caps. Insert shows an incurved margin in the caps.

The colors of the spores range from a light chocolate to a dark chocolate to purple brown. The stems are usually somewhat hollow with a fine pith.

Certain species such as *Psilocybe semilanceata*—the liberty cap—can be wrapped around the finger like a piece of string. Certain varieties have a dark purple ring around the top of the stem where the mushroom cap has detached itself from the stem. The purple-blackish color of the ring on the stems of some *Psilocybe* species is due to spores falling on the veil remnants attached to the stem after the cap of the mushrooms has opened.

Another predominant characteristic of several species in the *Psilocybe* genus is their ability to form wavy caps when the cap opens and the veil breaks. Certain species such as *Psilocybe cyanescens, Psilocybe ovoideocystidiata,* and *Psilocybe stuntzii* are good examples of species in the genera that do form a wavy cap. Even *Psilocybe cubensis* when grown indoors has produced a wavy cap. However, be weary. Always turn the cap over to make sure you have a *Psilocybe* species rather than a deadly species of *Galerina* because they also have wavy caps.

Psilocybe semilanceata with a striate margin—gill-lines showing through cap when moist.

All three of the active *Psilocybes* just mentioned above and three deadly species of *Galerina* macroscopically resemble one another and even mimic each other when growing together in the same mulched garden bed. They have been observed appearing under the caps of clusters of *Psilocybe cyanescens* and *Psilocybe stuntzii* in the Pacific Northwest of America.

Wavy-capped *Psilocybe cubensis* and *Psilocybe cyanescens*. Somewhat frosted *Psilocybe cyanescens* shows a striate margin. Inserts show incurved margins in both caps.

The color of the stems range from a pallid yellow or yellow-brown to olive brown while other species have pure white stems and some of those stems may have fine fibrils on the stems. Bluing on the white stemmed varieties usually occurs very fast when handled and is quite intense. In some regions, certain species have been known to occur throughout the year depending on their locations and climatic environments.

TWENTY

Psilocybe semilanceata

I scoured Oregon for almost two years, traveling hundreds of miles, walking past my prize, while looking in manure for *Psilocybe cubensis*. In the early 1970s, the only book available on magic mushrooms was F. C. Ghouled's, *Field Guide to the Psilocybin Mushroom*.

Ghouled intended his book be used to identify a few species of the divine mushrooms found in the southeastern United States; primarily in Florida and Texas. It is ironic that because all the while I was looking in manure for *Psilocybe cubensis*, I was walking past and the liberty caps I was seeking. Then in the fall of 1974, quite by accident, I learned of Lester Hale's shroom farm and his fields of divine mushrooms, the famed 'liberty cap' species—*Psilocybe semilanceata*—that I thought were *Psilocybe pelliculosa*.

Michael Engström

Psilocybe semilanceata

Psilocybe semilanceata

Cap: The cap of *Psilocybe semilanceata* ranges in size from 75-2.5 cm broad. It is twice as tall and conic with a profuse nipple. The color of the cap is variable from a rusty-brown hue to a pale yellow when dried. The margin of this species is often striate and translucent when moist with a sticky gelatinous pellicle—a layer of film that can be easily separated from the skin of the mushroom when moist.

Gills: The gills are adnate to adnexed and crowded appearing from a light chocolate brown to purple brown in age. Sometimes this species may produce gills that are of a whitish hue which indicates sterility in the specimen. The gill color appears to be much darker than *Psilocybe pelliculosa* and they ascend directly from the stripe into the cap.

Stem: The length and thickness of the stem ranges from 40-100 mm long. It appears to be of a pale to rusty brown color. The stem is also noted for its tough pith which is usually crooked and can be wrapped around ones finger like a piece of string, not breaking into splinters when wrapped around ones finger. Sometimes this species will stain blue after human handling, however that is usually rare.

Spores: 12-14 x 7-8 μ.

Spore Print: The color of the spore print for this species is dark purple brown.

Habitat: *Psilocybe semilanceata* grows scattered to gregarious in pasture lands but not growing directly in manure. Also in some European countries and the Pacific Northwest of the United States, this species along with a similar macroscopic species, *Psilocybe strictipes*—formerly known as *Psilocybe callosa*, can be found in newer well-fertilized

Psilocybe semilanceata

manicured lawns, fields, or other grassy areas, especially where cattle and sheep graze. They commonly grow in open fields in Oregon State with an epicenter of growth along the I-5 Corridor of the Willamette Valley region from Roseburg to Eugene and Corvallis, Oregon to the coastal region.

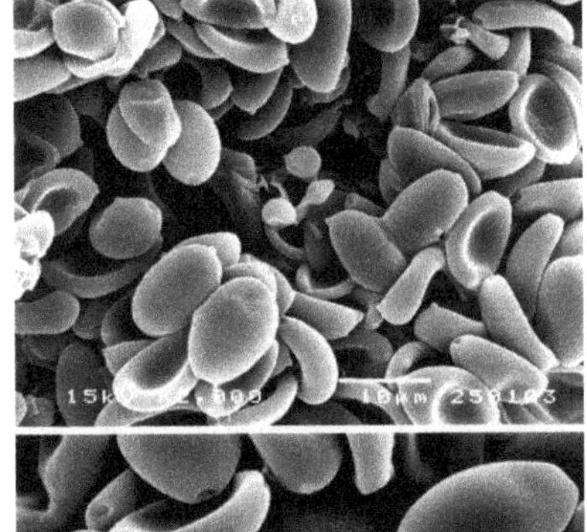

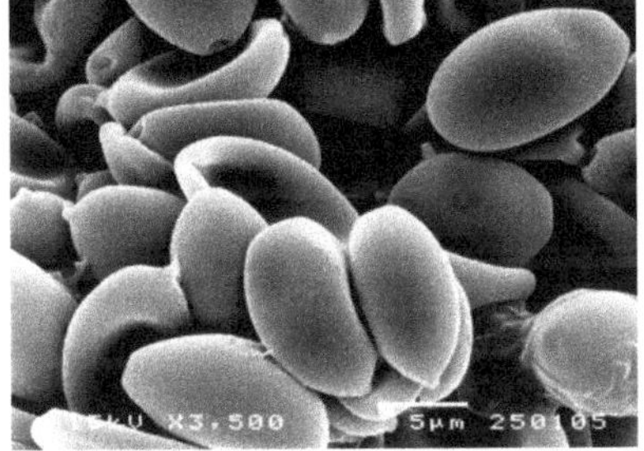

Prakitsin Sihanonth.

SEM Scanning Electron Microscopy—of *Psilocybe semilanceata*.

Both species have been collected from golf courses along the Oregon Coast and in the Seattle Arboretum. *Psilocybe semilanceata* is found around the base of sedge grass clumps and other tall rank grasses in pasture lands, open meadows, high school sporting areas, and in soccer fields and public parks in the PNW. Sometimes they appear in newly sodded lawns for one to two seasons if the lawns have perpetual lawn service care.

Distribution: Their distribution in the Pacific Northwest ranges from Northern California to British Columbia, Canada, west of the Cascades and along the coastal areas of Washington, Oregon and northern California. On occasion, this species can be found on new condo lawns in residential housing projects and golf courses along the coastal regions of the PNW and in northern New York State. In Canada, this species occurs as far north as Quebec City and in Southern Ontario to New Brunswick, Nova Scotia, Prince Edward Island and Newfoundland on the East Coast of Canada and in British Colombia on the West Coast of Canada.

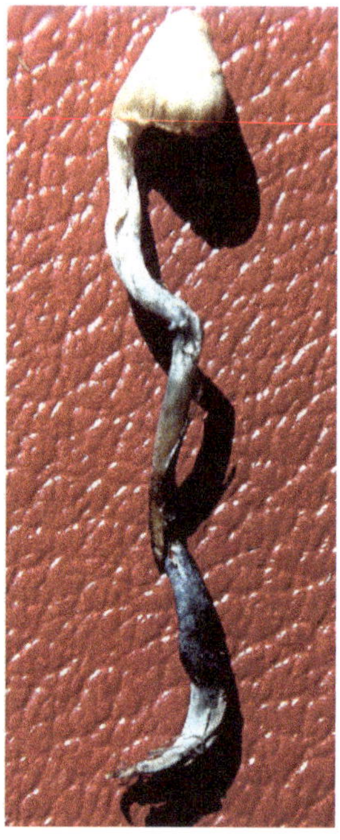

Bluing in *Psilocybe semilanceata*—rare.

This species has a cosmopolitan distribution and is known of in the UK, throughout Europe, Eastern Europe, Some Baltic and Serbian regions, Russia, India (Pune), Australia along the Gold Coast and New Zealand. This species has also been reported from Peru but not verified.

Season: In the Pacific Northwest United States and most European countries, *Psilocybe semilanceata* fruits from mid-August through November-December. In some locations, it may fruit as early as May and disappear until the fall and it usually ends when the winter frost or freeze begins and if those weather conditions only last a few days, and it warms up, liberty caps have been known to still occur, but not abundantly in January or early February. If the freeze begins and does last for more than three days then the shrooms are gone for the season.

Dosage: Several field guide published in the 1970s list the dosages for *Psilocybe semilanceata* as from 20 to 40 fresh mushrooms or from 1 to 1.5 grams dried. That would be the equivalent of somewhere between 30 to 40 doses to a fresh pound or approximately 60 dried powdered individual double-ought gelatin-capsuled (500 milligrams ea.) doses per dried ounce. Two triple-ought gelatin capsules are the equiv-

Swiss "liberty cap" postcard, circa 1960s.

alent to 1-dried gram of powder. Chemically, a single 1 gram dose of 2-500 milligram capsules of powdered material contains approximately 15 to 30 milligrams of the actual tryptamine alkaloids psilocybine and psilocine. That is also close to the dosage used in controlled studies of the effects in clinical studies with human volunteers.

"Liberty cap" card painted by Wipaporn in Thailand.

For those who wish to experience a first voyage with liberty cap mushrooms and have a pleasant rewarding experience, a dosage of 20 to 25 medium sized fresh mushrooms is suggested, with 15-25 minutes to digest the dosage. It is good to consume the fresh mushrooms while drinking a pint of Darigold or Nestles chocolate milk. The milk helps coat the stomach lining and keeps bacteria from harming one's neurological system. Two to three days later, a larger dosage of say 40 fresh specimens or 1.5 dried grams would provide the most rewarding experience.

• • • • •

In Latin, *Psilocybe semilanceata* translates as bald head—half speared. I translate the word psilo as naked rather than bald. So *psilo* is bald or naked and *cybe* is head. *Semilanceata* translates to *semi* for half and *lanceata* is spear or speared, which is easy to translate because the syllable of lance is easy to approach from an entomological linguistic point of view.

The generic epithet for *Psilocybe semilanceata* is liberty cap or caps. That epithet is derived from association with the French cap of liberty, the "Phrygian Bonnet", a symbol of the French Revolution. as shown on some coins minted during that period. It was known to users in the British Isles during the 1970s who called them both "liberty caps" and "pixie caps".

According to alternative medicine guru, Dr. Andrew Weil, he wrote in his book, *The Marriage of the Sun and the Moon,* that the hat symbol in turn derives from the Phrygian bonnet of Roman times, given to slaves upon emancipation. The *Oxford English Language Dictionary* describes the Phrygian bonnet as "a conical cap with the peak bent or turned over in the front, worn by the ancient Phrygians and in modern times identified with the cap of liberty."

When this species dries, it takes on the appearance of that ancient symbol. During the early 1970s, liberty cap mushrooms collected in Eugene, Oregon and as far west from Central Oregon to the Oregon Coast, claimed that liberty cap mushrooms resembled the Liberty Bell in Philadelphia. They did not get their name the Liberty Bell but from early patriots. Peter Stafford, author of the *Psychedelic Encyclopedia* noted the name of the liberty cap as being a symbol of the French Revolution and that the mushrooms resembled caps worn by patriots during and after the French Revolution.

The first public announcement of the presence of *Psilocybe semilanceata* in North America occurred in 1966 after the Royal Mountain Police seized mushrooms they found during a drug raid on a house of hippies and college students in Vancouver, British Colombia.

In 1975, Andrew Weill contributed a fantastic three part series on Mushroom Hunting in Oregon published in the *Journal of Altered States of Consciousness*. This article was so popular that it was reprinted in the *Journal of Psychedelic Drugs* and later in 1980 again reprinted in Dr. Weil's best seller, *The Marriage of the Sun and Moon*. In his

Jochen Gartz.

Sculpture with a hat resembling a liberty cap with a Native American face in Astoria, Oregon.

narrative Dr. Weil mentioned the Vancouver raid and then relates to the reader, how he sought out and bio-assayed the famed liberty cap species while in Oregon. His article on mushroom hunting in Oregon was the first written report on the presence of *Psilocybe semilanceata* in the Pacific Northwest of North America.

Although the primary habitats for *Psilocybe semilanceata* are manured soiled pasture lands and meadows with tall-rank wild grasses, this species on occasion has also been collected in the Seattle, Washington arboretum and from lawns on golf courses along the Oregon and northern California coastal region. During the past 40-year or more it has appeared in the lawns of numerous local school soccer fields in the Pacific Northwestern United States. As noted previously, it is macroscopically similar to *Psilocybe strictipes* but has a taller stripe. Sometimes found on lawns in the PNW, it is also very common on public lawns in parks in the UK, parks in Germany and various similar habitats located throughout the European, Scandinavian, Russian and Baltic communities of Europe.

TWENTY-ONE

Psilocybe allenii

In 2012, an unidentified species of *Psilocybe* was named in honor of my 38-years of research into the use and history of entheogenic mushrooms. That species, *Psilocybe allenii* took more than 5-years of collections, herbarium deposits, SEM photography before DNA proved it to be a new unnamed species.

Prior to the publication of the naming of the species with its taxonomic specifics, *Psilocybe allenii* was considered to be a very rare species and somewhat sporadic in its once-in-a-while sudden appearance in garden beds at local parks and along road areas mulched with alder and other hardwoods. Because it was an unknown species, it was not of interest or importance to many mycologists when it began spreading throughout the region. Its range of growth extended from the Bay of San Francisco to as far north as British Colombia, Canada.

Psilocybe allenii with striate margins on the caps and a purplish spore deposit on the grass.

This new species boasts small to medium sized caps that range in size from ¼ inch to 2 inches in di-

Bluing due to damage to the 'shrooms.

ameter and rarely become larger. They appear to be broadly convex to plane when mature in age, often becoming close to being hemispheric and not umbonate as they are sometimes slightly depressed in the center. They have a striate margin, sometimes slightly incurved and the cap does not become wavy like *Psilocybe cyanescens.*

Many fresh specimens, during and after a rainfall, will not reveal a striate margin in the young but more so in older mature specimens because they brown in age. When the mushrooms have not opened their veil while in their youthful stage, once moistened, there are visible striations continuing one fifth to half way towards the center of the cap.

Like most species of *Psilocybe,* their caps are hygrophanous, always changing color as they dry, changing from a bright yellowish color to a yellowish-orange color; varying in young wet specimens from a bright yellowish-orange to an orangey-brown, and then becoming very brown as they dry and age in the sun.

The surface is very smooth and viscid when moist. In aging, they change from a caramel brown to a light yellow-brown shade that eventually become the usual straw-yellow color that is common in many species of *Psilocybe* as they dry.

The intense bluing—oxidation of psilocine—is caused as the mushrooms are being picked. The damage that causes the stems to be splintered, as shown in the above photo, occurs when the mushrooms were still wet from morning due or a sprinkling of scattered rainfall. Likely the harvester attempted to lift the slippery and slimy 'shrooms from their mycelial roots and as they did so, the mucous texture of the 'shrooms splintered apart at the stem when improperly lifted from the ground.

Gill side of a young cap.

When moist from rain, the caps and stems are almost impossible to handle. They become very slippery, making it hard to hold on to the stem without causing oxidation from squeezing them.

When harvesters use two first-fingers to lift mushrooms from their mycelial roots, the applied pressure of the fingers on the mushrooms when lifting them from the topsoil, causes the stems to split apart from the cap. Then the snapped stems to splinter into several sections.

It is this type of accidental damage to the stem that causes the bluing oxidation of psilocine from this species to be released into the atmosphere. When the harvester touches the other mushrooms in the image, they will bruise blue almost instantly.

Psilocybe allenii in grassy wood-chip mulched.

The gills on the younger specimens of *Psilocybe allenii* are cream colored to pale gray brown, changing in color with age to a dark purple brown when mature. The margin of the gills are pale to whitish appearing to be a light grayish color when young and eventually becoming purplish brown in age with white edges.

The stems on *Psilocybe allenii* range in size from 4-7 cm. long by 2-4 mm. thick. They are straight and cylindrical and like many *Psilocybe* species, they have a hollow stem, which also stains strongly blue where damaged. The stem is rather firm and whitish when young. When checking on the base of the stem you can see that it is slightly enlarged at its base and very thick white rhizomorphs strands can still be seen in the photo.

Alan Rockefeller

Bluing in *Psilocybe allenii.*

The stems surface is smooth and sometimes silky and fibrillose; strongly bruising blue when bruised or damaged from human handling or naturally occurring damage. When wet they are slippery and hard to lift from the ground as noted above. Its mycelium is rhizomorphic and stains to an azures sky-blue when damaged. Its odor and taste is strongly farinaceous.

The spores of *Psilocybe allenii* are ellipsoid in shape and range in size from 11-1 to 14.2 by 6.5 to 7.9 μ. The spores of *Psilocybe allenii* are dark purple brown in color. This species is found on wood-chipped landscaping areas in cities. Common among public mulched garden areas and nurseries layered in alder and other hard wood mulches such as *Pinus radiata* (pine), *Quercus*, Eucalyptus., *Pseudotsuga menziesii,* and *Alnus* (alder) chips.

They are found in abundance in the wood-chipped gardens of homes, office buildings, new restaurants and apartment/condo complexes. Other locations for finding them are in the garden beds of public schools, and in city parks in both urban and suburban locations in the Pacific Northwest.

The fruiting bodies appear to be collybiod and are rather variable, depending on substrate quality and environmental conditions. This species is easy to cultivate on agar, grain spawn and sawdust or woodchips. It is a cold weather species that fruits abundantly from late September through January. *Psilocybe allenii* is very common in Northwestern America..

In the early 1980s, a few avid aficionados of the sacred mushrooms were aware of this species, reporting that it occasionally appeared in small colonies of wood chip landscaping in Northern California. The first public display of *Psilocybe allenii*—as an unidentified species of *Psilocybe*, occurred at one of the early Myco-Media annual mushroom workshops held at Breittenbush Hot Springs in Lake Detroit, Oregon. This species distribution occurs primarily along the I-5 Corridor from the bay area of San Francisco north to British Colombia, Canada.

This newly named species has a much wider distribution than originally reported. Collections have been harvested in mulched areas of Los Angeles to the southern urban regions of British Columbia, Canada. While primary Californian collections are abundant in public parks and most mulched roadways, Alan Rockefeller notes that the species is common in the Bay Area and Humboldt County of California, usually within 10 miles of the ocean or bay. It has also been reported as occurring at least 100 miles inland in California.

The season for finding *Psilocybe allenii* has different parameters depending on what state one lives in. In the San Francisoc Bay Area this it can be observed from late October through January, yet in the Puget Sound region of Seattle, it appears in late October through mid-December or until the 1st hard frost hits the region.

The normal dosage for *Psilocybe allenii* is from 1 large fresh specimen or from 2 to 5 small to medium sized specimens. When dried the average dose range is from 1 to 1.5 grams.

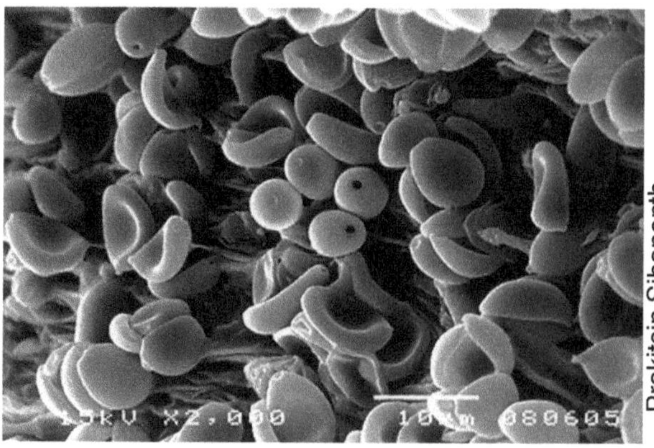

Prakitsin Sihanonth.

SEM of *Psilocybe allenii.*

One year a massive mulched area of I-5 between Eureka/Arcata, California boasted a humongous display of *Psilocybe cyanescens* and *Psilocybe*

Psilocybe allenii with slug or worm at base.

allenii on both sides of the Interstate. Those two species have been observed fruiting in a variety of local garden mulch composed of alder and willow chip compost, made up entirely with crushed and partial portions of broken twigs, stems, branches and smashed bark. Awareness of *Psilocybe allenii* was made public by several participants at some of the early 1980s Breitenbush, Oregon's Annual Mushroom Workshop Symposiums.

In David Arora's first edition of *Mushrooms Demystified*, *Psilocybe allenii* was misidentified in a Paul Stamets photograph as *Psilocybe cyanescens*. Then I mistakenly identified is, based on identification from Jeremy Bigwood as *Psilocybe cyanofibrillosa*.

This species was named in honor of me for my persistent belief that (1) it was indeed a new species, (2) the fact that I researched and deposited the first collections for scientific studies and (3) for my 38-years of contributions in the field of ethnomycology.

My investigation took three years. I first collected what is now *Psilocybe allenii* in 1982 in Seattle at a nursing home off Broadway on Capital Hill. There was a singular clump that was about 12 inches in diameter and about 5 inches in height. At first I assumed it was not a magic species. Then I saw blue tinges towards the bottom edges of some of the outer caps. It was so perfectly symmetrical in shape that from faraway it appeared as a single giant mushroom.

I had no camera with me at the time, so I was unable to record the size and shape of this magnificent clumped body of mushrooms. In the evening I separated the mushrooms from their base. There were 137 mushrooms in the cluster that I was able to spread out on paper to dry. That evening I ate three. It was the second most intense visual voyage I had ever undertaken. Over the years I only found small collections every year until I moved

Cluster of Psilocybe allenii with insect on center cap.

and left the city. I never found more than a half of a fresh pound in a single location at that time. This was indeed a rare species in Seattle that had not yet taken root but was very common in the San Francisco Bay Area.

Early in the Century, I harvested numerous collections from two locations in Seattle. Each season during that period I send those specimens to several colleagues that I worked with in the past. I sent specimens on three occasions to Dr. Gastón Guzmán of the Instituto de Ecologia in Veracruz, Mexico, along with photographs of the species and the specifics of the discovery.

Dr. Guzmán is the world's leading authority on sacred mushrooms of Mexico, the taxonomy of the genus *Psilocybe,* as well as the Indians who still use them in ritual healing and curing ceremonies. Dr. Guzmán told me he examined the dried specimens under the microscope and informed me that they were *Psilocybe cyanescens*.

I knew they were a macroscopically different species than *Psilocybe cyanescens*. I had a hard time understanding why Dr. Guzmán believed them to be *Psilocybe cyanescens.* However, it turns out that both species have the same spore-size range with one another. So after I sent that first collection to Dr. Guzmán I sent samples to Germany, Hawaii, and to

Art rendition of *Psilocybe allenii.*

Chulalongkorn University in Bangkok. I corresponded with Jan Borovîcka in Prague, Czech Republic, who offered to do the DNA sequencing in order to verify that I did indeed have a new unnamed species.

I sent specimens to Dr. Borovîcka for analysis to make sure his findings were correct. When the identification of the species was positively identified as a new species, I sent the macroscopic descriptions of this species to Dr. Borovîcka at the University of Prague and he, along with Alan Rockefeller and Peter G. Werner wrote the taxonomy of the species, which appeared in print in December of 2012. In short, that paper took a total of more than five years of research in order to have it published.

TWENTY-TWO

The 'Cyclone' Mushroom

Psilocybe azurescens was named by Paul Stamets and Jochen Gartz. In the late 1970s, a young mushroom enthusiast from Oregon, Paxton Hoag, brought his discovery of what he believed to be a new unidentified potent cold weather species of *Psilocybe* to the attention of the mushroom community. A new species had been discovered growing in the sand dunes of Hammond and Astoria, Oregon known as *Psilocybe azurescens*. Paxton presented his find at the 2nd International Conference on Hallucinogenic Mushrooms held at Fort Worden in Port Angeles, Washington.

Later Paxton hand-delivered a herbarium specimens to Dr. Gastón Guzmán for further study, believing it to be a new species. At the time, the mushroom was referred to as the "Astoria Mushroom". In the 1980s, Steven Peele of the Florida Mycology Research Center received samples, which he called *Psilocybe Astoria Ossip*. Consequently until the mid-1990s most who collected this species referred to it as *Psilocybe astoriensis*. During this period, Paxton became quite the cultivator of edible, medicinal, and other species of wild mushrooms. The mushroom was finally named for Paul Stamets' son Azureus and for the intense bluing reaction when the mushroom is damaged from human handling or from natural causes.

We have to thank Paxton and his friend Mark Herke of Astoria for their contribution to the studies of this species. Paxton introduced specimens of the species at early conferences and workshops on hallucinogenic fungi held in the Pacific Northwest. These conferences were specifically intended to bring to the

Psilocybe azurescens from Astoria, Oregon.

attention of the world, the history and re-discovery of what, in 1957, *Life* magazine had referred to as "mushrooms that caused strange visions." Back in the 1990s, Paxton shared some of that information to a friend of mine from the Nederland who wrote to me about the species.

Now I would like to provide some of my own input into this tale of the "Flying Saucer" or "Cyclone" *Psilocybe*—as it is sometimes called.

Psilocybe azurescens has been successfully transplanted into other mulched areas with similar environments but after 1-3 years of annual flushes, it tends to disappears and does not return.

When transplanted, *Psilocybe azurescens* grows somewhat differently in appearance from when they are in their natural sand dune or alder mulch habitat in the Pacific Northwestern United States. In his field guide, *Psilocybin Mushrooms of the World,* Stamets noted that *Psilocybe azurescens* was successfully transplanted into garden areas where the mushroom was not known to occur in a natural outdoor habitat.

Those transplants were limited to California, New Mexico, Ohio, Wisconsin and Vermont. Yet after a couple of years, those transplanted patches failed to produce new annual fruiting's and *Psilocybe azurescens* did not reappear or spread into other areas near where the transplanted patches had been created.

Bluing in *Psilocybe azurescens.*

European chemist and cultivator of the sacred mushrooms, Dr. Jochen Gartz at the University of Leipzig in Germany transplanted several patches of mycelium obtained by him and I from collections we harvested in the fall of 1990 in Astoria, Oregon. I had given Dr. Gartz obtained prints of *Psilocybe azurescens* from me in the late 1980s.

In the 1990s Dr. Gartz had successfully grown the species in small patches located in both public and private garden areas of Leipzig, Germany. He expressed his interest in studying the species in a natural outdoor transplant of it through more than a dozen letters of communication with him while at the Department of Fungal Biotransformation at the University of Leipzig, Germany.

After traveling with Dr. Gartz in the Pacific Northwest for three weeks, we were fortunate to catch up with my friends in Oregon who took us to their patches of *Psilocybe azurescens.* We collected many species while in Oregon, which we mailed back to Germany so that Dr. Gartz was able to successfully grow several patches of *Psilocybe azurescens* using methods as described in Stamets and Chilton's *The Mushroom Cultivator.*

When the nutrients in the soil and/or wood chip habitats are gone, so are the mushrooms. It is not good to rely on stories by amateur forages of wild mushrooms who claim to have found species appearing in States where certain species are generally not found.

Psilocybe azurescens

Cap: The caps are 3-10 cm broad and are conic to convex in shape, usually expanding broadly overnight. They are flat with age with a pronounced umbo—or protrude—with a smooth surface and are often viscid when moist with a separate pellicle that implies that when the mushroom is wet from rain, the lines of the

Bluing in *Psilocybe azurescens.*

gills can be seen on the top of the cap. Most Psilocybes have a separate pellicle, which is a clear skin like substance that can be separated and lifted from the mush when moist. The caps color is from a dull chestnut to caramel, often bruising blue to blue black when damaged.

Gills: The gills ascend to the stem and are sinuate to adnate. The colors of the gills appear to be a light brown and are mottled with white edges.

Stem: The length of the stem ranges in size from 90-200 mm long x 3-6 mm thick. It has a silky white-like stem that is fibrous with little specks of mycelium. The base of the stem thickens downwards and at times is often curved. There is instant staining blue where bruised.

Spores: The spore sizes range from 12-13.5 x 6.8 μ.

Spore Print: The spores are of a dark purplish black color.

Habitat: The mushrooms grow from cespitose to gregarious, fruiting abundantly on deciduous hardwood chips of alder, willow, eucalyptus and other hardwoods as well as in sandy soils rich in lignicolous debris. This species was first reported in the early 1980s as common in the sand dunes along the Northern coastal region of Astoria and Hammond, Oregon in dune grasses.

Distribution: Although this species is common along the northern coast of Oregon in dune grasses, it also is found in wood chipped garden beds from northern California to British Columbia, Canada.

Season: September to December.

Dosage: Extremely potent. 1 large fresh mushroom or from 2 to 4 small medium specimens or 1 dried gram of powdered pooled material into a single double-ought capsule will suffice for a most rewarding experience. Always remember to take 15-30 minutes to consume the dosage in order to prevent a fast come on to the effects of the mushrooms. And remember that set and setting also helps those who are interested in trying this potent *Psilocybe* species to have a most enjoyable experience.

In a private communication to me, Paxton Hoag spoke of his participation at Port Townsend in 1977 when he met with Jonathan Ott. He informed me that he attended a Microscopy Workshop and showed Dr. Guzman a specimen of *Psilocybe azurescens*.

Nothing came of that visit and Hoag next attended a mushroom workshop of Stamets in Florence, Oregon where he made arrangements to send Dr. Guzman a collection to be deposited at the herbarium for further study. Hoag mentioned that he holds to the *Psilocybe azurescens* name as being the ones from the waterfront in Astoria, although it was called *Psilocybe astoriensis* for many years.

TWENTY-THREE

Mystery of *Psilocybe baeocystis*

Psilocybe baeocystis is a potent when fresh. It instantly stains intensely blue when damaged from human handling. Lawn mower blades leave blue stems rising at the top of the mowed grass where *Psilocybe baeocystis* once grew.

Although this species is quite potent when fresh, it tends to loses much of its potency when dried. Occasionally this species has been very abundant, and then it disappears for many years with only small patches occurring from mid to late summer in lawns, in public parks and on school playgrounds and soccer fields.

Psilocybe baeocystis occurs in lawns and can be found in alder mulched garden beds; fruiting alongside *Psilocybe cyanescens* and *Psilocybe stuntzii.* On occasion, *Psilocybe baeocystis* has been known to grow in the early fall alongside of *Psilocybe ovoideocystidiata*.

Caleb Brown

Psilocybe baeocystis woodchip variety.

The reason *Psilocybe baeocystis* and many of the more potent cold-weather *psilocybian* species are not so common at times is due to the closure of clear cuts in the Pacific Northwest. In the late 1990s to early 2000s, more than 85% of the clear cuts in the Pacific Northwest became illegal. It is from the clear cuts that the alder wood chips—twigs, stems and branches—originate and are transported to local landscaping firms who, in turn, supply the wood chips to local garden shops in the Pacific Northwest.

While *Psilocybe baeocystis, Psilocybe stuntzii*, and similar species are pasture land fungi, mostly occurring naturally in the manured soil of cattle and sometimes horse-manured fields. They are rare in their natural habitat. When the manured-soil of such pastures are used to make liquid or compost made fertilizers used on newly sodded lawns, even seeded lawns, as well as soils in mulched gardens with the liquid fertilizers or manured topsoil overlaid with wood chips, this combination of conditions allow *Psilocybe baeocystis* to appear in high abundance in the Pacific Northwest from Bandon Oregon to Vancouver, British Colombia, Canada; East and West along the I-5 Corridor.

Psilocybe baeocystis

Cap: The cap of *Psilocybe baeocystis* ranges in size from 1.5 cm to 5.5 cm broad to an olive-brown color in age to a straw-yellow color that is convex to conic in its shape. The cap appears to be translucent when moist and the edges appear to be somewhat pleated towards the bottom portion of the caps edge, often intensely staining blue to blue-green when damaged.

Gills: The gills of the cap are attached in mature specimens. The color of the gills are a dark purple-grey with white edges.

Stem: The stem of this species ranges in size from 50-70 x 2-3 mm long. The stems color is of a white crème to yellow towards the top. It appears to be covered with white filaments.

Spores: The spores of this species ranges in size from 10-13.2 x 6.2-7 μ.

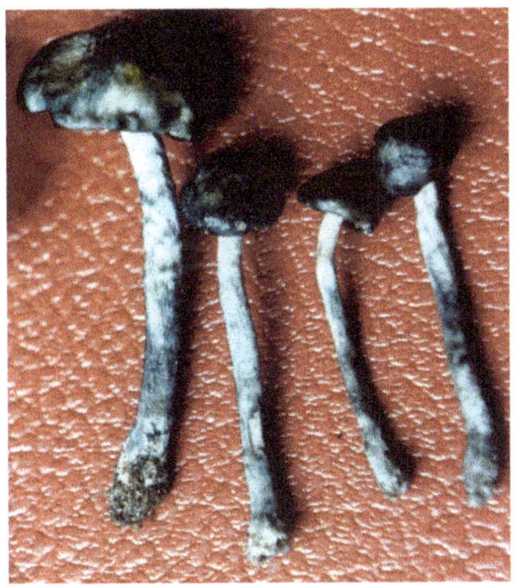

Psilocybe baeocystis bluing as harvested.

Spore Print: The color of the spores of *Psilocybe baeocystis* are purple grey.

Habitat: *Psilocybe baeocystis* was discovered in Eugene, Oregon in 1945. This species was considered to be rare during the 1970s and 80s. Then appeared commonly and abundant in city parks, and dozens of gardens surrounding Bank of America branches in the Pacific Northwest. The mushroom is believed to have spread when banks used a local product of wood chips known as Steer-Co, which were Alder Chips from the same garden supply firm in the Seattle region of the Pacific Northwest. This was short lived and by the summer of 1986, it was again considered rare in the Puget Sound Region. Now it is common in garden bed boxes in the downtown area of Seattle, Washington

Psilocybe baeocystis appears in the soil of mulched garden beds, fruiting around the base areas under rhododendrons and rose bushes; sometimes growing in amongst groupings of *Psilocybe stuntzii* in lawns and with *Psilocybe cyanescens* in alder mulched garden beds. *Psilocybe baeocystis* grows abundantly in lawns or grassy areas rich in humus or lignin and/or in alder wood chips and bark mulched garden beds in public locations in the Pacific Northwest.

Distribution: From Eugene, Oregon to Seattle, Washington, up to British Columbia, Canada. Once considered rare, then common, *Psilocybe baeocystis* is now again uncommon. It may appear occasionally in public gardens and the gardens of well-kept apartment and condo lawns of many cities along the I-5 corridor between San

Francisco, California north to British Colombia, Canada. There have been unsubstantiated reports of *Psilocybe baeocystis* in the Northeastern Coastal area of the United States.

Season: June to October in lawns. From late September through December and sometimes into January in mulched garden beds.

Dosage: 1 to 2 large mushroom specimens or from 2 to 4 small specimens.

The reason *Psilocybe baeocystis* is considered rare again is because alder chips commonly obtained from logging clear cut sites in the Oregon and Washington region of the Pacific Northwest are now illegal. Because of the low stock of alder many cold weather *Psilocybe* species are not as common today as they were 20-years-ago.

In the early 1960s, *Psilocybe baeocystis* was labeled in many field guides on mushroom identification as toxic/hallucinogenic, poisonous/hallucinogenic or with warnings that it was deadly to children. This occurred after two children, one in Washington, the other in California died after allegedly consuming this species in a meal prepared by their parents.

In the Washington case, mushroom specimens were collected from the lawn of the family and identified by Dr. Rolf Singer, at the time, the curator of Chicago's Field Museum of Natural History. A few years earlier in 1958, Dr. Singer, along with Dr. Alexander H. Smith of the University of Michigan wrote the monograph on the genus *Psilocybe.* There were errors in the identification of some species presented in the monograph.

Spider hatchlings on gill-plates.

Fresh harvest of lawn *Psilocybe baeocystis.*

I reread the original paper published on this sad incident involving psilocybian fungi and realized that something was wrong in the identification of the species after viewing the photograph in the medical journal. The image looked like *Psilocybe cyanescens* and not *Psilocybe baeocystis.* The child in Washington had eaten *Psilocybe cyanescens*, which caused his death. Thus I was able to determine that the child did not die from consuming *Psilocybe baeocystis*.

Many mushroom aficionados experienced problems breathing and thought they were dying after eating *Psilocybe baeocystis.* Some reported having experienced extreme muscle dis-coordination and being unable to walk and probably had eaten more mushrooms than their bodies needed.

I received a copy of the article, along with one of the three photographs of the mushrooms collected on the child's front lawn. Sure enough, the poisonous mushroom was not *Psilocybe baeocystis* as identified by Dr. Singer that had caused the death of the child. Because of that incident, most mushroom identification manuals and field guides list *Psilocybe baeocystis*s with warnings that it was dangerous to children.

TWENTY-FOUR

Wavy Capped Psilocybe

In the late 1970s, 18 fresh specimens of *Psilocybe cyanescens* were harvested in the wild alongside a logging road in a clear cut in Kingston, Washington. This species was common and abundant in most garden bed boxes in the five and ½ acre Freeway Park in downtown Seattle. They took over in most of the downtown park's many garden bed boxes; often growing in association along with colonies of *Psilocybe baeocystis, Psilocybe stuntzii,* and *Psilocybe azurescens.* After three years, the nutrients in the mulched beds had been consumed by the massive mycelial underground network feeding off the woody debris composed substantially of alder chips known locally as 'Steer-Co.'

Not only were they in the mulch beds, but *Psilocybe stuntzii, Psilocybe baeocystis* and even liberty caps—*Psilocybe semilanceata*—were common in park lawns.

In fact, most of downtown Seattle's office buildings and restaurants with lawns or mulched garden areas had large colonies of *Psilocybe cyanescens* and other active species that were common in such environments from the 1970s through 2010.

Psilocybe cyanescens with wavy cap.

Since the fall of 2010, many areas in the Puget Sound where annual crops of *Psilocybe cyanescens* grew for decades were

Psilocybe cyanescens with blue and green stains.

disappearing as a result of over picking. In the Pacific Northwest, *Psilocybe cyanescens* can still be observed in many public locations.

Psilocybe cyanescens fruits annually each fall, but only for a period of two to three years then they disappear. The lack of fertilizers and replenishing of the alder chips has declined because most property owners eventually cannot afford to pay landscaping firms to continue providing perpetual lawn care service to the garden lawns and mulched areas.

Psilocybe cyanescens

Cap: The size of the cap of *Psilocybe cyanescens* ranges from 2-4 (5) cm broad to up to two inches or wider in diameter. The caps shape are conic to conic-convex eventually expanding to broadly convex and is plain in age with a wavy margin. The color of the cap is chestnut to caramel with age and like all Psilocybes, it is also hygrophanous; that is they change color in both age and drying, causing the color of the cap to become a yellowish-brown or ochraceous color. It is viscid when moist. The caps color when damaged bruises a deep bluish to sometimes bluish-green color when the oxidative bluing color mixes with the straw-yellowish color of the drying cap, thus creating a deep sea turtle-green color along the edges of the cap.

Gills: The gills are somewhat adnate to subdecurrent in shape and are very broad. The color of the gills appear to be a light cinnamon brown to a deep smoky brown while their edges appear to be paler.

Stem: The stem ranges in size from 20-80 mm long by 2.3-5.5 mm thick. The stem may be somewhat curved and appear to have an enlarged base. The color of the stem is white with fine fibrils scattered vertically up and down the stem, which often stains blue to blue indigo-black when damaged. Like many *Psilocybe* species, the stem is hollow, yet it is hard to see its hollowness.

Spores: The spores range in size from 9-12 x 5.8 μ.

Spore Print: The spores of *Psilocybe cyanescens* are a dark purple brown color while the gills appear to be a light cinnamon-brown color when young.

Habitat: Scattered in humus enriched in woody debris among leaves and twigs, alder wood chips and alder bark mulch. Often growing solitary by clusters and clumps in heavily mulched areas with rhododendrons or rose bushes, ivy, strawberry plants and they also love to feed off of Blackberry brambles The fungi *Spinellus fusiger* grows as a parasitic mold on mushrooms and is best avoided.

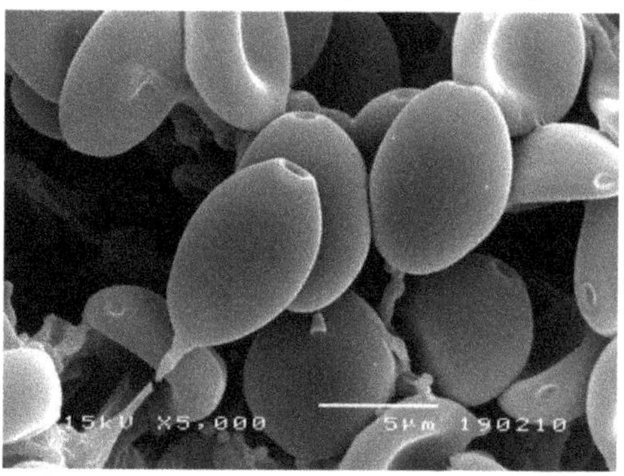

SEM of *Psilocybe cyanescens.*

Prakitsin Sihanonth.

At times, *Psilocybe cyanescens* is found in well-fertilized lawns and in grassy areas next to mulched garden beds. Lawn care service providers who mow grassy lawn areas often crop the edges of the mushrooms growing along the edges of the beds, which helps spread the spores of the fungi. They are common in public areas such as parks, at schools, at office buildings and on well-manicured lawns and mulched garden areas of both urban and suburban apartments/condos and residential homes.

Distribution: San Francisco, California to British Columbia, Canada. Although this species is rare in the wild, it is abundant in man-made environments throughout the Pacific Northwest. Sometimes more than 20 to 50 pounds may appear in a single location.

Season: September through December from Oregon to British Colombia, Canada, and from mid to late October through January in the San Francisco Bay Area.

Dosage: The young specimens of *Psilocybe cyanescens* are the most potent of species. One large fresh specimen or two to three small to medium sized specimens when fresh are good for the most rewarding experience. When fresh, an ounce of *Psilocybe cyanescens* contains as many as 4-6 large specimens—enough to set 4-6 individuals on the path to enlightenment. However, if one collects an ounce of *Psilocybe cyanescens* of the younger smaller thick specimens, you could have 15 to 30 small mushrooms that weigh in at one ounce fresh. Care should be taken when eating this species because 15-30 small mushrooms can be from 10 to 15 doses.

A good 15-30 minutes is needed when consuming this species for visual effects. Consume slowly. One fresh pound could contain 40 to 60 doses. A dried ounce of pooled specimens of *Psilocybe cyanescens* can be powdered and put into double-ought gelatin capsules, with each capsule holding 500 milligrams mushrooms. Each person will have a dosage equivalent to a Mazatec dosage as used in archaic traditional healing and curing ceremonies. This is as many as seven fresh specimens of different sizes of *Psilocybe caerulescens* or 12 pairs of *Psilocybe mexicana*—normal dosages.

Psilocybe cyanescens infected with *Spinellus fusiger*, a parasitic mold.

TWENTY-FIVE

Bluing Coastal Ovoids

Currently the most common and widespread psilocybian mushroom in the United States is a recently described new species of magic mushroom that occurs on both coasts of the country. This new species has been named *Psilocybe ovoideo-cystidiata.* It is common on both coasts It was first reported by Dr. Gastón Guzmán, Richard V. Gaines and Florencia Ramírez-Guillén from three collections harvested by Richard V. Gaines in Montgomery County, east of Evansburg, at Evansburg State Park, Pennsylvania on June 5, 2005. In 2007 they published the taxonomy on the species in a prestigious academic journal.

At the time it was not known to occur elsewhere. In 2007, I along with Dr. Prakitsin Sihanonth of Chulalongkorn University in Bangkok, Dr. Jochen Gartz of the University of Leipzig and Dan Molter of Ohio, all reported the occurrence of this species from Bethany, Ohio, Pennsylvania and West Virginia.

Color changes in caps of *Psilocybe ovoideocystidiata.*

During the last five years this species has also now been positively identified from the West Coast of America, mostly from locations in the Pacific Northwest of the United States. However, the extent of its West Coast distribution ranges from San Diego to British Columbia, Canada along the I-5 corridor. It has also been reported from Central California as well.

Psilocybe ovoideocystidiata belongs to the section *Stuntzii*. It is macroscopically very similar in appearance to both *Psilocybe stuntzii* and *Psilocybe fimetaria*. All three have an annulus present or remnants of the veil that are visible and the cap and veil both tend to bruise blue when the cap is damaged from overnight temperature changes or when it opens and the veil breaks free of the cap.

One distinguishing characteristic of *Psilocybe ovoideocystidiata* is that after the cap breaks open the veil remnant never rises in height along with its stem. It always stays at the exact place where it opened up on the stem. On the other hand, the remaining veil remnant on both *Psilocybe stuntzi*i and *Psilocybe fimetaria*, always remaining close to the cap as the stem grows upwards. In the Midwest to the East Coast, ludible users who collect and bio-assay this species refer to them by the common name of 'blue foot,' an epithet used to describe another species, *Psilocybe caerulipes*. However, some are now calling them 'blue bells' and 'blue ringers.'

Of course, the average blue-ringer species in the PNW are *Psilocybe stuntzii* and *Psilocybe fimetaria*. The stem and veil's tend to grow upwards along with the cap. The species also has a habit of the caps staining intensely blue just from a slight drop in the evening temperature as seen in the photographs featured in this chapter.

Psilocybe ovoideocystidiata

Cap: (10-) 15-25 (-43) mm diam. Convex to subumbonate, translucent and striate at the margin. Hygrophanous, orangish brown to yellowish brown, sometimes whitish when dried.

Gills: Subadnate, brownish pale to a dark brownish-violaceous color that is somewhat even.

Stem: (15-) 25-60 (-90) X (1-) 2-5 (-7) mm, smooth to a floccose-scaly below and cylindrical and equal in shape. Sometimes with a bulbous base the stem is very hollow and usually has rhizomorphic white strands of mycelium around the base of the stem when detached from the wood chips in the ground. The context of the mycelium is white at the base is whitish and sometimes blues when damaged or from natural elements when picking this species from its wood chipped habitat.

Spores: (7-) 8-9 X (5.5-) 6-7 (-8.5) μ.

Spore Print: Violaceous dark.

Habitat: Scattered to gregarious in clusters, clumps and singularity, fruiting on wood and woody debris. Found along trails or places with herbaceous plants in deciduous forests and along streams and riverbanks which are the natural habitat for this species. On the west coast of America, this species appears in man-made environments in urban and suburban areas.

Distribution: According to Guzmán, this species was originally only known from the type species found in Montgomery County, east of Evansburg State Park, Pennsylvania. Also know to occur in Ohio, West Virginia, Pennsylvania and Michigan. Recent collections are now known to occur from the West Coast in northern California to British Colombia, Canada.

Season: Early spring and from mid-summer to late fall after rain.

Dosage: 2-3 doses per fresh ounce and one to two grams dried. This species has about the same potency as *Psilocybe stuntzii*; from 20 to 40 fresh mushrooms of various sizes.

Recently a good friend that I had met on Facebook came to visit me and we went to a park for lunch. As we gobbled down our fast food meal, he went over and looked into a mulch bed and began to giggle in excitement; asking me to come look at what he

Fresh Bluing young *Psilocybe ovoideocystidiata*

found in the mulch. I gathered from the sound of his voice that just maybe he had found some special mushrooms. OMG was he was excited.

Funny thing is he kind of let out a yelp like a puppy begging to have a doggie treat. For some reason or other, I know not? I knew from the sound of his voice that he must have found some magic in the brush of that mulched garden bed with a tree and lots of bushes.

So, being partially physically disabled at my age, I slowly hobbled over to see what had caused him to become so excited. There In the wood chips were dozens of small blue-capped fruiting bodies of close to three fresh ounces of *Psilocybe ovoideocystidiata*.

This is the same species that Richard V. Gaines had found in Pennsylvania in 2005 and Dan Molter and his friend Mushpuppet of the 'Shroomery collected in Bethany, Ohio. In 2010, I co-authored a paper with Dr. Prakitsin Sihanonth of Chulalongkorn University in Bangkok, Thailand, Dr. Jochen Gartz of the University of Leipzig in Germany and Dan Molter of Ohio on the occurrence, chemistry and cultivation of this species. And new locations are

Blue capped *Psilocybe ovoideocystidiata.*

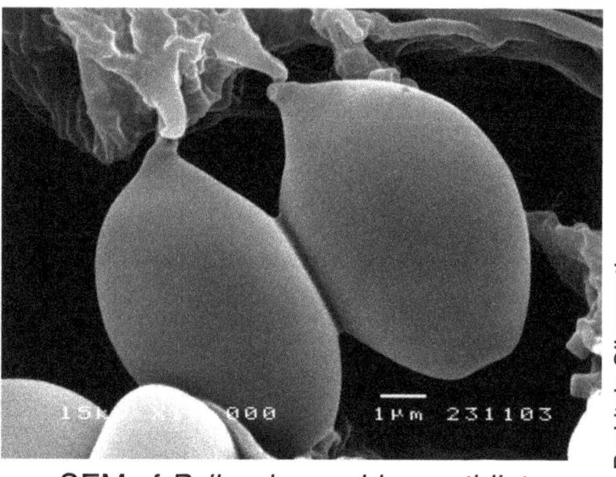

SEM of *Psilocybe ovoideocystidiata*

Prakitsin Sihanonth

constantly being reported on many of the online mushroom community website forums. During the past year, this species is now known to have been reported from Maine, Maryland, and Rhode Island and south along the East Coast of America, as well as San Diego, Sacramento, the Bay Area of San Francisco; and north to British Colombia, Canada.

In the spring of 2014, between April and June, this mushroom has become known to thousands of online ‘shroomers who frequent mushroom websites and are pleased to learn that there is a species of magic mushrooms they can find on both coastal regions of the United States, as well as in some Midwestern states.

In the mid-west USA, this species grows along flood plain regions in wild habitats, although it is now showing up in both urban and suburban areas of large metropolitan cities; appearing in mulched garden beds from late March through June and again later in the fall. However, if there is rain during the cooler summer months the species will grow in different states at different times.

I should mention that I believe that *Psilocybe ovoideocystidiata* has been on the West Coast of America for a few centuries or longer. It was here all this time but most people, especially me, thought that it was nothing more than a variation of *Psilocybe stuntzii*—‘blue ringers’. Since mid-April of 2014, mushroom foragers have been posting unbelievable photographs of their finds of this species from California north to Bellingham, Washington at Facebook’s numerous mushroom groups and at Google and other similar social media online communities.

TWENTY-SIX

King of the Blue Ringers

When I first moved to Seattle in the spring of 1974, I had asked myself over and over how was I going to find someone to take me out in the fall to pick mushrooms—liberty caps—in a pasture and where would the pastures be?

I was not aware of city mushrooms although when my family and I lived in Eugene we were aware of some species being collected in two public parks in the city. One was at the Rose Gardens at Skinner's Butte Park along the Willamette River, including Skinner's Butte Park, and the other was Hendricks Park at the southern tip of Eugene's University of Oregon's Campus heading towards Springfield, a sister city to Eugene.

So on the 4th of July, my wife was visiting her mother, sister and 3 brothers in Beaverton, Oregon and there I was sitting on the right side of the lawn to Seattle's Art Museum at Volunteer Park in Seattle.

I had been playing my guitar and smoking a doobie and as I mentioned above, thinking about magic mushroom hunting in the fall. After a few puffs I begin to play 'Broken Arrow' originally recorded by the Buffalo

. *Psilocybe stuntzii*—lawn variety

Springfield and sung by Neil Young. It was one of my favorite songs that I loved to sing while playing my guitar.

Looking down towards the grass nearby where I was sitting, I begin to notice a grouping of mushrooms and many growing singularly in the surrounding grass of the lawn around where I sat. The mushrooms appeared to have remnants of a veil—ring—on the stem near the cap and some of those veil remnants of several of the mushrooms appeared to be blue in color.

Too further my curiosity, I also noticed that some of the caps I saw had color changes that ranged from a brown color with a striate margin; having slowly in the sun, changed to a straw-yellow color and came to the realization that they actually resembled tiny versions of *Psilocybe cubensis.* So, I then began to pick the mushrooms I had found on the lawn.

Two years later, this species had not really been identified outside of the fact that it was a bluing *Psilocybe* not yet known to the academic community and only to a few in the counter culture movement. That was when I had found this species in gardens around campus buildings and many lawns of the University of Washington. I also learned over the next 5 years that this species also fruited throughout most of the year; depending solely on local weather conditions in the Puget Sound of Washington State. It was there at the UW that I brought my bag of mushrooms to the offices of Dr. Daniel Stuntz, hoping he could find the time to properly identify them for me.

When I first met with Dr. Stuntz, he was very cordial and polite, and more than willing to spend 20 minutes with me on the subject of psilocybian fungi. He decided to show me Drs. Rolf Singer and Alex-

Psilocybe stuntzii—wood-chip variety.

Bluing in *Psilocybe stuntzii*—lawn variety

ander H. Smith's monograph of the genus *Psilocybe.* This monograph described several species from the Pacific Northwest and Mexico with both macroscopic descriptions and line drawing sketches of the species they studied.

Dr. Stuntz looked through the article he had and we both looked at the generic description that fitted the macroscopic characteristics of my collected specimens. After we noticed the 'wavy cap' sketch of *Psilocybe cyanescens*, we both came to the conclusion that I had just harvested a nice collection of *Psilocybe cyanescens*—referred to by the epithet as 'wavy caps.'

Although at the time Dr. Stuntz had misidentified my mushrooms, I should point out that this species I had harvested from dozens of lawns that grew in the spring and summer; also came up in the fall in wood chipped garden beds was a new unidentified species.

Then in 1976, Dr. Gastón Guzmán and Jonathan Ott wrote the paper on the taxonomy of this species, naming the mushroom in honor of Dr. Stuntz as, *Psilocybe stuntzii*—'blue ringers'. Unfortunately, when Dr. Stuntz examined my mushrooms, we both failed to notice the presence of the veil remnants on *Psilocybe stuntzii*, a feature not found in *Psilocybe cyanescens*. Nor was there any mention in Singer and Smith's monograph that *Psilocybe cyanescens* had a veil remnant present on the stem of the species.

In the early 1980s, I met with Dr. Andrew Weil who was interested in the distribution of the known species of magic mushrooms that occurred in the Pacific Northwest. We had previously attended several conferences and workshops on magic mushrooms and I discretely informed him that I knew where there were lawns with that from a distance appeared to have carpets of magic mushrooms—three species at least—on them.

Dr. Weil was a very pleasant individual to meet with and he definitely was very sincere in his desire to learn everything he could about the various species and why they were so common. He also appreciated edible mushrooms as well as the psilocybian species. Prior to my meeting Dr. Weil, he had already authored some classic papers on the ludible use of these fungi amongst members of the counter culture. I had offered to share with Dr. Weil, my sacred hunting ground where there were lawns of *Psilocybe stuntzii* that ran for blocks at the South Center Shopping Mall in Tukwila, Washington; about 16 miles south of Seattle.

Please do not head out to Tukwila in search of these mushrooms. They are no longer there. It took me many years to learn why they were there. From Tukwila south to Kent and Auburn, Washington, there were dozens of pastures where once, hundreds of young adults during the 1970s were ticketed for trespassing while picking liberty caps. Most of those ludible users were not aware of other species. And within a ten-year-period, between 1970 and 1980, more than one dozen field guides and 6 cultivation manuals on these mushrooms suddenly appeared in print.

So for many years, lawns along sidewalks at the South Center Shopping Mall and Industrial Park, stretched the length of the Center on both sides of Andover East and Andover West since the early 1990s. However, The Evergreen Tree Service, no longer supplying lawn care service at the Mall or the Industrial Park. The mushrooms have disappeared because many of the nearby pastures are no longer there. They have been replaced, as noted previously in this narrative, with blocks of one-story non-polluting buildings, Boeing office. Once the pastures were gone, so was the compost and fertilizers used on those lawns; thus, no more shrooms on that parcel of land.

Handful of *Psilocybe stuntzii*—lawn variety

When Dr. Weil came to visit me and my family, I took him and his friends and we went to South Center in Tukwila and I showed him the mushrooms he was interested in meeting. Not just the lawns of 'blue ringers' but also two different locations where there were lawns that were abundant with hundreds of specimens of *Psilocybe baeocystis*. And while many thought that the baeos were rare, I had actually been collecting this species on these lawns for more than 6-years. On a few occasions, some lawns gave birth to *Psilocybe semilanceata*, but not on that trip.

Psilocybe stuntzii—lawn variety with insert

All in all, I can honestly say that this fungal foray had been a most successful mission. We had gathered herbarium specimens and were able to shoot some really beautiful photographs of *Psilocybe stuntzii* and *Psilocybe baeocystis.* Today both species still grow abundantly in the Pacific Northwest, but are rare in Seattle; appearing more commonly in suburban areas wherever there are new condos with newly sodded lawns, in the lawns of new restaurants, government buildings, hospitals, and on lawns in public parks.

Both species originate in pasture lands, but like liberty caps, they do not fruit directly in manure but apparently grow with their mycelial threads attached to the roots of wild grasses in manured soil. And of course, both species occur in garden beds of wood chips of alder and other mixed hardwoods in the fall months until the freeze or frost begins.

Psilocybe stuntzii

Cap: 1.5-5 cm broad. Obtusely conic, expanding to convex-umbonate or flat with age. Margin is striate and translucent when moist. Hygrophanous. Dark chestnut brown while lighter towards the center. Olive-greenish at times, fading to a pale yellowish brown or pale yellow. Viscid when moist from a gelatinous pellicle.

Gills: Adnate to adnexed, close to sub distant and moderately broad.

Stem: 30 to 60 mm long x 2-4 mm thick. Enlarged at base. remnants of a veil remain and are usually bluish from natural injury when the cap opens. With a whitish pith. Staining blue to blue-green where injured.

Spores: 9-12 x 55-8.3 x5-7.7 μ.

Spore Print: Dark purplish grayish brown.

Habitat: Growing gregarious to subcespitose in clusters and clumps, in conifer wood chips (alder wood), in soils rich in woody debris, in new lawns and fields of freshly laid sod. It seems this is a species found in manured soil in pastures in the PNW. However, this species is extremely rare in pastures and very abundant in man-made environments; on lawns and mulched garden bed habitats.

Distribution: San Francisco north to British Columbia, Canada.

Season: From late July through September in lawns and grassy areas and from late September through December in mulched garden beds.

Dosage: 20 to 30 fresh specimens, 1/3 fresh ounce or 1-3 dried grams.

TWENTY-SEVEN

The Derrumbe Mushroom

In his field guide, *Psilocybine Mushrooms of the World*, Stamets mentions that R. Gordon Wasson first ate 13 pairs of *Psilocybe caerulescens* during his initial velada with María Sabina. Actually, it was 13 pairs of small specimens of *Psilocybe caerulescens.*

The species was originally discovered and identified from Huntsville, Alabama in 1923 by mycologist, William Alfonso Murrill. Since then it had never been seen or collected in the United States or Alabama until the early 1990s when specimens were found in both Florida and Mississippi. In the late 1950s, R. Gordon Wasson and French mycologist, Roger Heim identified it as the derrumbe—landslide—mushroom of the Mazatec Indians.

Concerning the synonymy of *Psilocybe weilii* with that of *Psilocybe caerulescens*, it came about when Stamets collected specimens in Cherokee County, near Alpharetta, Georgia in 1995. At the time of its taxonomic study, Dr. Guzmán said that *Psilocybe weilii* was delimited from that of *Psilocybe caerulescens* due to the presence of pleurocystidia in the former.

Alan Rockefeller.

Psilocybe caerulescens.

In 1997, Dr. Guzmán, Fidel Tapia and Paul Stamets published their findings and named the species in honor of Professor Andrew Weil from the University of Arizona's College of Medicine, in recognition of his studies on hallucinogenic fungi

Psilocybe caerulescens

Cap: The cap of this species ranges in diameter from 2.5 to 9 cm. The color of the cap may stain a deep sea green to black cinnamon to rust. It is also cone shaped when young, expanding in age. The margin is slightly incurved in young and the cap is hygrophanous. Staining blue to deep-sea-green.

Gills: Close. Light cinnamon to brown becoming light to dark in age with white edges.

Stem: 3.5 to 10 cm. Long. Cream colored. Hollow with fibrous hairs, veil falls off early in young stages.

Spores: The spores of *Psilocybe caerulescens* range in size from 7-10 X 4.5 μ. They are ellipsoid in shape.

Spore Print: Dark purplish brown in deposit.

Habitat: Gregarious to cespitose, rarely solitary and often in clusters and clumps. On disturbed grounds devoid of herbaceous plants. This species prefers mudslides, orange brown soils, and sugar cane soils, in sugar cane mulch and landslide areas along sugarcane roads. In northern Georgia, *Psilocybe caerulescens* was found fruiting under Loblolly Pine and Sweet Gum and sometimes it had been harvested in Bermuda grass or fescue, often in red clay soil that is enriched with pine needles. They also grow in urban lawns and in the deep woods on areas where decaying wood collects. I

Alan Rockefeller.

Psilocybe caerulescens.

have seen some from Georgia in thick swampy areas.

Derrumbe's blue-green staining cap.

Distribution: Georgia, Florida, Mississippi, Louisiana, Alabama, Mexico, Panama, Venezuela and Brazil.

Season: Late spring—May—through the summer months into the early fall—September—depending on the location. In the 1990s, *Psilocybe caerulescens* was collected from South Carolina and Northern Georgia as *Psilocybe weilii.* Other collections of *Psilocybe caerulescens* have been reported from Florida, Alabama and Mississippi.

Those particular southern States, Louisiana, Alabama and Mississippi have the same climatic conditions and the same ecosystem as in the Mexican State of Oaxaca. *Psilocybe caerulescens* occurs in the early spring through summer into September—the rainy season, while in the Mexican State of Oaxaca, the rainy season begins in late May to early June, extending through September.

Dosage: 1 to 7 fresh mushrooms of various sizes. One large or 2-5 to 7 smaller specimens.

I posted a lengthy pictorial at the Shroomery and at Mycotopia in the earl 2000s in their popular online mushroom community forums with my concerns that *Psilocybe weilii* could be the same mushroom as *Psilocybe caerulescens*. I compared both species with numerous photos and research notes that suggested that *Psilocybe weilii* was likely *Psilocybe caerulescens*. My obser-vaitons have since been validated.

TWENTY-EIGHT

Psilocybe mexicana

Psilocybe mexicana was first described in 1956 by French mycologist Roger Heim from three collections he and Wasson made in 1953 in Oaxaca, Mexico. They were collected during one of Heim's expeditions with the Wasson's to participate in a ceremony with María Sabina in the mid-1950s. Almost twenty years later, Drs. Gaston Gueman and Steven H. Pollock described a related species as *Psilocybe tampanensis.* This new species was discovered by Dr. Pollock and Gary Lincoff in Tampa, Florida. Since that find of a songle specimen, no one found again it in the USA.

Here's the back story on the Mexicana species evolution. While attending a boring mycological conference in Tampa, Florida, Gary Lincoff had just finished co-authoring *Toxic and Hallucinogenic Mushroom Poisoning*, which was due out that fall. Lincoff was not yet a mycologist and had not yet published his *Audubon Mushroom Field Guide*. He specifically wanted to attend a presentation on *Psilocybe* species presented by the world's leading authority of the genera, Dr. Gastón Guzmán. Lincoff was interested in

Alan Rockefeller.

Psilocybe mexicana.

their possible use as treatments in psychiatric medicine.

Psilocybe mexicana.

While attending the conference, Lincoff met Dr. Steven Pollock, a physician and mycologist who had a mushroom laboratory in his Winnebago to examine mushrooms and creative cultures for later studies. Both instantly became very close friends.

They decided to take a break from the boredom of the mycological conference to check out the local flora and fauna east of Brandon, near Tampa. During the foray, the intrepid 'shroom seekers came upon what they believe was an unidentified species of *Psilocybe*. They harvested a single specimen from sandy soiled grassy meadow habitat. A year later in the summer of 1978, Drs. Guzmán and Pollock published their findings on the taxonomy of the new species; naming it *Psilocybe tampanensis* after the city it was found near.

Since the time of its discovery by Steven Pollock and Gary Lincoff, *Psilocybe tampanensis* had never been re-collected in Florida; however, it was later observed in the wild one other time in a 1996 collection found by Dr. Guzmán in Mississippi.

In a misleading story about *Psilocybe tampanensis*, Hamilton Morris described in "Blood Spore: Of Murder and Mushrooms", a featured in the vice rag, *Harper's Magazine*—not to be confused with the national syndicated publication, *Harper's Bazaar*.

According to Morris, in 1995 Steven Peele, curator of Florida Mycology Research Center curator, had inoculated bales of hay with spores of *Psilocybe tampanensis* ahead of Hurricane Erin and Opal. Morris wrote that in the aftermath of Hurricanes spores from Peele's inoculated hay had been disbursed throughout the entire southeastern United States.

Yet, in the same narrative, Morris described how Dr. Guzmán had found a single specimen of *Psilocybe tampanensis* in Mississippi in 1995; and a year later, another specimen fruiting on Bagasse in Louisiana. Apparently Morris misread Guzmán's paper on the *Psilocybe* species found in Mississippi and Louisiana. The Louisiana specimens Dr. Guzmán described were a non-active species, *Psilocybe pseudobullacea,* a synonym for *Psilocybe pegleriana.* Morris reported sightings in Atlanta and Southern Georgia of *Psilocybe tampanensis*—which are being re-identified as *Psilocybe mexicana.*

Apparently Peele and Morris were not aware that all of the mushrooms in the Southeastern United States previously identified as *Psilocybe tampanensis* and *Psilocybe galindoi,* are most likely synonyms of *Psilocybe mexicana.* However, Alan Rockerfeller believes that DNA sequencing is needed to verify the synonomy of *p.mexicana* with *pitampanesis.*

In a private correspondence, Dr. Guzmán learned that through microscopic examinations that *Psilocybe tampanensis* and another newly named species identified from Florida, *Psilocybe galindoi* were synonymous with *Psilocybe mexicana.*

Distribution of *Psilocybe mexicana* is more widespread than originally thought. I believe that it is not as rare as it was once believed and likely occurs from Texas to Florida and North to Southern Georgia. *Psilocybe mexicana* is common in most of subtropical Mexico and in Guatemala in habitats similar to those in the South to Sourtheastn USA.

Psilocybe mexicana

Cap: Approximately .5-3 cm broad. Conic to campanulate to convex when mature. Usually displaying a small umbo or protrude. Even and striate at margin halfway towards the center of the cap. Hygrophanous and ochraceous brown to orangey to straw-brown or yellowish-gray to pale in drying. Sometimes there is bluing at the margin. Bluing occurs in age or when damaged from human handling.

Gills: Adnate to adnexed and at times sinuate. Pale gray to dark purple-brown with white edges.

Stem: 40 to 125 mm long by 1-3 mm thick. Equal but slightly thickened at the base. The stem appears to be a straw-yellow to brownish color, becoming darker in age or where the stem has been bruised. Veil is inconspicuous in the adult fruiting bodies. Bruising blue where injured.

Spores: (8-9.9) X 5.5-7.7 (8) **μ**. With a distinct germ pore and a short appendage.

Spore Print: Dark purple-brown to black-purplish brown in their deposit.

Habitat: Solitary to gregarious in meadows, horse pastures and in soil rich in manure, and in sandy soil in a meadow. Never directly in manure.

Distribution: In the United States (Florida, Mississippi and Georgia); Mexico at elevations of 1000 to 1500 meters altitude, Michoacán, Morelos, Jalisco, Oaxaca, Puebla, Western Xalapa, Veracruz, Mexico; and in Guatemala.

Season: Original Pollock collection occurred in Florida in September of 1977. It can be found fruiting in subtropical Mexico from June through September and in the same season for Guatemala.

Dosage: One gram dried. 20 or more fresh specimens.

In Spring 1978, Steven Pollock grew a crop of *Psilocybe tampanensis—Psilocybe mexicana* in a backyard greenhouse from the single culture he and Lincoff found during their break form the mycological conference the previous fall and presented to Dr. Guzmán as the original type species found near Tampa, Florida.

Hans Grootewall.

1000-gram package of *Psilocybe mexicana* sclerotia.

Pollock grew robust specimens that sporulated copiously with caps as wide as 38 mm in diameter and stems that were thick and reached as high as 60 mm in length.

Pollock's sclerotia became popular in the Netherland mushroom scene, being sold as the *Psilocybe tampanensis* 'truffle'. Another new species from Florida, *Psilocybe galindoi,* was also recognized as a synonym of *Psilocybe mexicana.* Other 'shrooms sold in the Netherland have been labeled with non-existing names like *Psilocybe Hollandia* and *Psilocybe MacKennae.* They are also the sclerotia of *Psilocybe mexicana*, Psilocybian mushrooms were rendered illegal in the Nederland in 2008. However, the sclerotia from psilocybian fungi was not included in the banned substance law; nor were spores or growing kits made illegal. The Dutch Parliament banned more than 186 species of these divine mushrooms. Because of the lawmakers' ignorance of drug laws and mycology, their ban on magic mushrooms included several edible species originally posted in a paper authored by Drs. Guzman and Gartz and myself.

Index

Other World Names for Entheogenic Fungi

Austria: schwämmerln gegessen (mad mushrooms).
Bali: jamur tahi sapi (magic mushrooms).
legelain (dizziness).
Central Africa: (Banzu people): losulu.
China: hsiao chun (laughter mushroom).
hsiao:ho (laughter).
Denmark: Spids Nøgenhat (pointy naked-hat).
Fiji: nui-ni-tevoro (devils parasol).
Germany: narrenschwämme (foolish mushroom).
Honduras: suntiama for *Psilocybe cubensis*.
Hungary: bolond gomba (fool's mushroom).
Italy: funghetti.
Ivory Coast: (Mao people): tamu (mushroom of knowledge).
Japan: maitake (dancing mushroom).
waraitake (laughing mushroom).
o-waraitake (big laughing mushroom).
odoritake (jumping mushroom).
shibiretake (numbing mushroom).
waraitake modoki (?).
Nederland: kaalkopje (bald-head),
paddo and/or paddos (mushrooms and/or magic mushrooms).
New Guinea: koull tourroum, koobltourrum.
Slovakia: zalené huby (mad mushroom).
szmer (szalec-foolish).
Lysohlávky (Psilocybes),
divé huby (mad/crazy/wild mushrooms),
muchotrávka červená (Amanita muscaria).
Spain: sorgin zorrotz (witch's thread).
Sweden: toppisar or toppslätsskivling for *Psilocybe semi lanceata.*
Thailand: hed kee kwai (mushroom which appears after water buffalo defecates).
hed kee wua (mushroom which appears after cow defecates).
Refers to both Thai *Psilocybe cubensis* and *Copelan dia* species in manure.
Zaire: (Eala people): abanda.

Bibliography

Allen, John W. and Jochen Gartz. *Teonanácatl: A Bibliography of Entheogenic Fungi,* 2008.

Arora, David. *Mushrooms Demystified,* 2 ed., Ten Speed Press, 1981.

de Rios, Marlene Dobkin. *Hallucinogens: Cross-CulturalPperspectives*, Univ New Mexico Press, 1984.

de Rios, Marlene Dobkin. *The Wilderness of Mind: Sacred Plants in Cross-Cultural Perspective*, Sage Publications, 1976.

Finkelstein, Nat, "Hongi Meester", *Psychedelic Review*, 1968, Vol. 10:52-63

Graves, Robert. "Mushrooms, Food of the Gods" Review of *Mushrooms, Russia, and History,* by Valentina Pavlovna Wasson, R. Gordon Wasson, *Atlantic Monthly,* Aug, 1957, pp. 73-79.

Guzman, Gaston. *The Genus Psilocybe: A Systematic Revision of the Known Species Including the History, Distribution, and Chemistry of the Hallucinogenic Species*, J. Cramer, 1983

Leary, Timothy. *High Priest*, Ronin, 1995.

Lincoff, Gary H. *The Audubon Society Field Guide to North American Mushrooms,* Alfred A. Knopf, 1981.

Lincoff, Gary H. and D. H. Mitchel. *Toxic and Hallucinogenic Mushroom Poisoning: A Handbook for Physicians and Mushroom Hunters,* Van Nostrand Reinhold, 1978.

Lincoln, John One Man's Mexico: A Record of Travels and Encounters, Century Publishing, 1967.

Morris, Hamilton. "Blood Spore: Of Murder and Mushrooms", *Harper's Magazine*, July, 2013

_____ *The Oxford English Dictionary*, Second Edition, Oxford Univ Press, 1987.

_____ *Panaeolina foenisecii, High Times,* Oct., 1988.

Riedlinger, Thomas J. *The Sacred Mushroom Seeker: Essays for R. Gordon Wasson*. Portland: Dioscorides Press, 1990.

Smith, David E. (ed) Journal of Psychedelic Drugs, Haight-Ashbury Publications, 1967-76.

Stafford, Peter. *Psychedelic Encyclopedia,* Ronin, 1993.

Stamets, Paul. *Psilocybin Mushrooms of the World: An Identification Guide,* Ten Speed Press, 1996.

Wasson, R. Gordon, Stella Kramrisch, Jonathan Ott, and Carl A. P. Ruck. *Persephone's Quest: Entheogens and the Origins of Religion*. Yale University Press, 1986.

Wasson, R. Gordon. *The Wondrous Mushroom: Mycolatry in Mesoamerica*. New York: McGraw-Hill, 1980.

Wasson, R. Gordon. *Maria Sabina and Her Mazatec Mushroom Velada*. New York: Harcourt, 1976.

Wasson, R. Gordon. *Soma: Divine Mushroom of Immortality*. 1968.

Wasson, R. Gordon. "Seeking the Magic Mushrooms," *Life* magazine, May 13, 1957.

Weil, Andrew T. "Mushroom Hunting in Oregon," *J. Altered States of Consciousness*, Baywood Publishing, 1976, pg. 279.

Weil, Andrew, T. *The Marriage of the Sun and the Moon,* Mariner Books, 1981.

Suggested Reading

Allen, J. W. 1997 [1076]. *Magic Mushrooms of the Pacific Northwest* Psilly Publications and RaverBooks, Seattle, Washington. 12 color photos. 36 black and white.

Allen, J. W. 1998. *Magic Mushrooms of the Hawaiian Islands*. Psilly Publications and RaverBooks. Seattle, Washington. Color Photos.

Allen, J. W. 1999. Magic Mushrooms of Australia and New Zealand. Www.erowid.org/library/books_online/magic_mushrooms_aunz.shtml/

Allen, J. W. and J. Arthur. 2004. Ethnomycology and Distribution of the Psilocybian Mushrooms. In: Metzner, Ralph (Editor, with Diane Conn Darling). *Teonanácatl: Sacred Mushroom of Vision*. Four Trees Press. Green Earth Foundation. El Verano, California. 297pages. See pages 49-66.

Allen, J. W. 2007. Fresh Mushrooms: A tour of the world's largest producer of Magic Mushrooms. *Heads* Online, vol. 7(5):32-36.

Estrada, A. 1976. *Maria Sabina: Her Life, Her Chants. An Autobiography*. Ross-Erikson. California.

Furst, P. T. 1986. *Psychedelic Fungi. Encyclopedia of Psychoactive Drugs*. Chelsea House Publishing. New York.

Gartz, J. 1997-98. *Magic Mushrooms Around the World: A Scientific Journey Across Cultures and Time. The case for Challenging Research and Value Systems*. Translated from the masterpiece "*Narremschwammer*" by C. Taake.

Guzmán, G., Allen, J. W. and J. Gartz. 2000. A Worldwide Geographical Distribution of the Neurotropic Fungi, an Analysis and Discussion. *Anali dei Museo Civico* vol. 14:189-280. Rovereto, Italy. (214 species described and 39 images).

Hofmann, A. 1980. *LSD My Problem Child*. McGraw-Hill. New York. Translated from German to English by Jonathan Ott.

Leary, T. 1995[1968]. *High Priest*. Ronin Publications Inc. Berkeley, California.

Leary, T. 1983. *Flashbacks: A Personal and Cultural History of an Era*. J. P. Tarcher Inc. Los Angeles.

Letcher, A. 2007. *Shroom: A Cultural History of the Magic Mushroom*. ECCO. An imprint of Harper Collins Publishers. New York.

Lincoff, G. and D. H. Mitchell (Eds.). 1980. *Toxic and Hallucinogenic Mushrooms*. Van Nostrand Reinhold. New York.

McKenna, T. 1993. *Food of the Gods: The Search for The Original Tree of Life*. Bantam Books. New York.

Menser, G. P. 1977 [1997]. *Hallucinogenic and Poisonous Mushroom Field Guide*. Published and Distributed by Ronin Publishing. Oakland, California.

Nicholas, L. G. and Kerry Ogamé. 2006. *Psilocybin Mushroom Handbook: Easy Indoor and Outdoor Cultivation*. Lux Natura. Quick American. Canada.

Ott, J. 1976 [1979]. *Hallucinogenic Plants of North America*. Wingbow press. Berkeley, California.

Ott, J. 1993. *Pharmacotheon: Entheogenic Drugs, Their Plant Sources and History*. (see pp273-319. Natural Products Co. Kennewick, Washington.

Ott, J. and J. Bigwood (Eds.). 1978. *Teonanacatl: Hallucinogenic Mushrooms of North America*. Madrona Press. Seattle, Washington.

Penner, J. [Editor]. 2013. *Timothy Leary The Harvard Years*. Early writings on LSD and Psilocybin with Richaerd Alpert, Huston Smith, Ralph Metzner, and Others. Park Street Press. Rochester, Vermont.

Reidlinger, T. J. (Ed.). 1990. *The Sacred Mushroom Seeker: Essays for R. Gordon Wasson*. Dioscorides Press. Portland, Oregon.

Rumack, Barry and David G. Spoerke. 1994. *Handbook of Mushroom poisoning: Diagnosis and Treatment*. CRC Press. Boca Raton, Ann Arbor, London, Tokyo. 464 Pages.

Sanford, J. 1966. *In Search of the Magic Mushroom*. Clarkson N. Porter. New York.

Schultes, R. E. 1978. *Hallucinogenic Plants*. A Golden Garden Guide. Golden Press. New York.

Schultes, R. E., Hofmann, A. and Christian Rätsch. 2001. *Plants of the Gods*. McGraw-Hill Book Co. New York.

Stafford, P. 2003. *Magic Mushrooms*. Ronin Publishing. Oakland, California.

Stamets, P. 1996. *A Field Guide to Psilocybin Mushrooms of the World*. Ten Speed Press. Berkeley, California.

Trout, K., and Friends. [Keeper of the Trout and Friends]. 2007. *Some Simple Tryptamines*. 2nd Edition. Mydriatic Productions. Moksha Press. Miami, Florida. Printed in China.
Trout's Notes #FS-X7 Revised 12-2006 with Minor Revisions 5-2007. Full color photographs. Includes *Bufo alvarius* toads and their alkaloidal gland compounds.

Wasson, R. G. May 13, 1957. *Life* magazine.

Wasson, R. G. 1980. *The Wondrous Mushroom: Mycolatry in Mesoamerica*. McGraw-Hill Book Co. New York.

Weil, A. 1972. *The Natural Mind: A New Way of Looking at Drugs and the Higher Consciousness*. Houghton Mifflin. Boston, Ma.

Weil, A. 1980. *Marriage of the Sun and Moon*. Houghton Mifflin. Boston, Ma.

Weninger, Joseph,. 2012. *Psychoactive Mushrooms of the Pacific Northwest*. Outskirts Press. Parker, Colorado. Paperback: 158 pages. Color photographs. July 16.

Author Bio

John W. Allen—Mushroom John is an amateur ethnomycologist who has studied, photographed and lectured on entheogenic fungi for more than 40 years. He is the author of 11 books, one medical poster, three CD-ROMs of mushroom data *(Teonanácatl: A bibliography of Entheogenic Mushrooms, Mushroom Pioneers and Psilocybian Mushroom Cultivation: A Brief History*), One Psychedelic Inspired Art CD-ROM (1060 graphic designs) and many additional articles appearing in academic journals and ephemeral publications on the non-traditional uses and field identification of psychoactive fungi in the Pacific Northwest of North America, Australia, New Zealand, Thailand, Cambodia, Malaysia, Europe, Great Britain and Scandinavia. During his studies on the sacred Mushrooms, Allen also has presented over 100 lectures and slide presentation, discovered a new species, *Psilocybe samuiensis* Guzmán, Bandala and Allen, and recently a new species was named in his honor, *Psilocybe allenii,* Borovičkîa, Rockefeller and P. G. Werner. Allen's latest journal, *Ethnomycological Journals: Sacred Mushroom Studies* Vol. 9 is posted online at http://www.maps.org/books/Neuro-MasterApril20-2013.pdf/ Currently Allen provides two great websites pertaining to psilocybian mushrooms, Mushroom John's Shroom World: http://www.mushroomjohn.org/ and three mushroom groups at http://www.facebook.com/ as John W. Allen. Allen resides in the Pacific Northwestern United States.

CPSIA information can be obtained
at www.ICGtesting.com
Printed in the USA
JSHW010945090322
23725JS00002B/2